Contents

Travel to Landmarks

The Red Fort, Delhi

Louise Nicholson
Photographs by Francesco Venturi

Tauris Parke Books, London

For Giles

The author and photographer would particularly like to thank the Taj Group of hotels for their hospitality while researching this book, and especially Ravi Dubey and Sharon Dick. They are also indebted to Nalini Thakur for her encouragement, and to Francesca Bristol, Dionne Daniel and Reggie Kumar.

Published by Tauris Parke Books
110 Gloucester Avenue, London NW1 8JA
In association with KEA Publishing Services Ltd, London

Travel to Landmarks

Series Editor: Judy Spours
Designers: Sharon Ellis and Paul West
Original plans and maps by Anindita Mitra and Jaideep Chakrabati
All photographs by Francesco Venturi except:
Nicolas Sapieha, pages 6, 46, 54, 86; Victoria and Albert Museum, pages 8, 26, 108; British Museum, page 33

British Library Cataloguing in Publication Data
Nicholson, Louise, 1954 May 1–
  The Red Fort, Delhi, – (Travel to Landmarks series).
  1. India (Republic). Delhi – Visitors' guides
  1. Title 11. Series
  915.4'560452

ISBN 1-85043-173-6

Photosetting by Westerham Press
Colour separation by Fabbri, Milan, Italy
Printed by Fabbri, Milan, Italy

Red Fort, Delhi

Introduction

'It first occurred to the omniscient mind that he should select on the banks of the aforesaid river some pleasant site, distinguished by its genial climate, where he might found a splendid fort and delightful edifices, agreeably to the promptings of his generous heart, through which streams of water should be made to flow, and the terraces of which should overlook the river.' Muhammad Tahir, Inayat Khan *Shahjahan-nama*, 1657–58.

Such worthy thoughts, according to the royal librarian, prompted the Mughal Emperor Shah Jahan to found a fresh city at Delhi in the mid-seventeenth century. He called it Shahjahanabad, meaning City of Shah Jahan. At its centre stood the Red Fort, a vast walled complex of beautiful palaces and meeting halls from which the Emperor ruled with unmatched public pomp and ceremony. Today, the surviving Fort buildings stand silently amid the still bustling city, now called Old Delhi.

The Red Fort's success was instant. It represented the pinnacle of Mughal palace-fort building, and symbolized political and economic power. It was also perhaps the most extravagant and sophisticated theatre ever built for daily performances of one of the world's most dazzlingly grand courts. But its glory was short-lived; as the Mughal Empire waned, so did the Fort. Later Emperors abused the fine buildings, raiders snatched its treasures, marauders wrecked its buildings and finally the British, blind to its qualities, pulled down the greater part. Even this century, what remains has been largely ignored, unappreciated and uncared for. But, despite the ravages of time and human action, the extraordinary achievement of the Red Fort in plan and fine architecture is still visible today, although it is unjustly ignored. It is time to set the record straight, to look again at the surviving buildings and to bring the Fort alive through the personality of its creator, Shah Jahan, and his Court.

The Red Fort and its surrounding city constitute the only large-scale Mughal city planned and built from scratch to survive as a living city. Built in just over nine years, it burst into life in 1648 and, although the palace buildings are peopled only by ghosts, the city it supported still thrives today and the inhabitants of its tiny lanes are often descendants of merchants and craftsmen who served Shah Jahan and his Court, still practising the same trades in the same areas. Here they live and work, shop in the markets and celebrate their festivals in the streets. And a few old families

The sun softens on a great marble pier of the most extravagant Red Fort building, the Diwan-i-Khas, highlighting the boldly carved foliage of the capital and base, the panel of floral inlay bereft of its blossom stones, the two perfectly proportioned cartouche panels above, and the crisply cut cusps of the arch. Across the courtyard stands the Khas Mahal.

This watercolour of the Red Fort seen from the far bank of the Yamuna River was painted by a Company School artist at Delhi in about 1836. Although the hey-day of Mughal life was over, the British destruction is still two decades away. The Fort is crammed with buildings and it is easy to imagine them bustling with Mughal Court life. Almost half of the cool riverside is devoted to the harem. Starting from the left, Azad Burj (Lion Tower) is followed by four harem buildings: Khurd Jahan (now gone), Jahanara Begum's mansion (surviving), Daria Mahal (now gone) and Rang Mahal (surviving). The Emperor's Khas Mahal is central, and its octagonal Mussaman Burj still has its gilded roof. After the Diwan-i-Khas and the Hammams to the right, the fine garden pavilion was soon to be replaced by Bahadur Shah II (ruled 1837–58) with two small pavilions. Finally, Shah Burj (King's Tower) is where the Nahr-i Bihisht canal entered the Fort, and the canopied cascade and pool added by Aurangzeb is also visible. In the background, the triple, gilded domes of Moti Masjid rise behind the Hammams, and between the great Lahore and Delhi gateways are the domes and minarets of Jama Masjid.

who a generation ago deserted the lanes for spacious, air-conditioned comfort in the New Delhi suburbs keep the family haveli (courtyard mansion) in Old Delhi and speak proudly of the city they come from, even if they have never slept a night in it.

The key to the Red Fort's success was firstly that it was designed not merely for Court pleasure. It may have contained glittering palaces, but it was also the power-base for the whole Empire, for internal government and external foreign affairs. It was built for defence, too, although this role would later prove its Achilles' Heel. The Red Fort was also a complete community, a city-within-a-city, with its own bazaars (the covered Chatta Chowk is a token survivor), gardens and mansions for favoured courtiers. Every detail of layout and every building reflected Mughal greatness, using the finest materials to realise the most mature Mughal designs.

Secondly, the supporting city was an essential part of the original plan. It had its own protective walls; its great mosque, the Jama Masjid (Friday Mosque), stands on the only hillock so all can see it; and its host of specialist bazaars, which supplied the vast Court with everything it needed from silk slippers to fresh Kabul melons. The city gained enough momentum to survive, albeit less glamorously, when the Mughal Empire waned and, more importantly, when the British built New Delhi and its competing shopping centre at nearby Connaught Place.

Thirdly, the whole of Shahjahanabad, both Red Fort and city, was a thoroughly royal undertaking. The city outside the Emperor's palace-fort was an extension of it in design, patronage and function. Indeed, Fort and city sustained one another, living in symbiosis. The Jama Masjid encapsulates the idea, for it was planned as the mosque for both the city and the royal Red Fort, which had no internal place of prayer. The city's main market street, Chandni Chowk, was laid out by one princess; additional markets, sarais (inns), Hammams (baths), mosques and gardens were given by other members of the royal family; and grand havelis (mansions) were built by favoured princes and courtiers. The havelis have mostly gone, but those markets and places of worship are still focuses of Old Delhi. Conversely, the public had access to the daily public meetings held in the Diwan-i-Am (Public Audience Hall) in the Fort itself, a fundamental element of Mughal rule.

As a royal undertaking, the Emperor's personal interest and vast finances were behind the project. With a stable empire and a huge income from taxes paid by his

Cartloads of sacks create a perpetual traffic jam outside the
wholesale spice market behind Fatehpuri Masjid. Above this timeless
scene, a large advertisement appeals to the modern housewife to buy
her boxes of ready-ground garam masala.

Opposite, buses arriving at sunrise can park on the flats where the Yamuna River's waters used to flow. The porters unload the roof, unaware of a Mughal glory behind them, the Azad Burj at the southern end of the Fort's riverfront.

Above, the Jama Masjid stands silhouetted on a hillock in Shahjahanabad, now known as Old Delhi, the city which lies to the west of the Red Fort and was conceived as an essential extension of it. Indeed, this was the mosque for the royal Court and the citizens, since none was originally planned for the Fort.

subjects, Shah Jahan could indulge his obsession, building a new and magnificent capital whose centrepiece would become a legend in his lifetime and whose magnificent planning and buildings would survive, in part, to be admired by posterity. Shah Jahan seems to have taken an active part in the design, direction and encouragement of the whole project. He was involved in the general plan and in the detailed designs for the marble palaces, the Chatta Chowk, the Jama Masjid and probably more. As one recorder noted, perhaps with an overdose of loyalty: 'Occasionally His Majesty supervised the work of goldsmiths, jewellers and sculptors. Thereupon specialists commissioned to design new buildings would submit their plans to His Majesty, who discussed them with expert persons . . . Various monuments, which even the best-versed architect could not have devised, were drawn up by His Majesty personally. His advice or his objections were regarded as binding.'

Forthly, the Red Fort and its city are an inspired triumph of urban planning. Within the Fort, the core of the design is T-shaped, the cross-bar consisting of a string of palaces facing the Yamuna's cool river breezes on the east side of the Fort. To the west, they face the main axis of the Fort and city: a procession of increasingly less private and less royal buildings which leads to a giant gateway, out of the seat of power and into the city's principal thoroughfare, Chandni Chowk.

Finally, each building in the Red Fort displays the hallmark of perfect taste and elegance. Built at the height of one of the most cultured courts the world has known, this is Mughal palace architecture at its most ambitious and sophisticated. Imagined in its original completeness, it would have easily outshone its contemporary European rival, Louis XIV's palace at Versailles, and it covered twice the area of the largest European palace, the Escorial. Of the surviving structures, each one perfectly fulfils its function. At the same time, each is visually satisfying, relates happily to its neighbours and fits snugly into the overall plan. Lines are simple, proportions human in scale, detailing restrained and both materials and workmanship of the highest quality. Architectural historian Percy Brown judged it in 1942 as 'the last and finest of those great citadels, representative of the Moslem power in India, the culmination of the experience in building such imperial retreats which had been developing for several centuries.' Thus the Red Fort symbolizes the apex of Mughal cultural refinement.

In assessing this extraordinary achievement, it is important to discover what, apart from his 'omniscient mind' and 'generous heart' prompted Shah Jahan to build a new capital city, and what enabled him to do it so well. He was the fifth Mughal emperor. The first was Babur, a Turk of the Burlas tribe. A poet, diarist, soldier, statesman and adventurer rolled into one, he was descended from two soldier heroes: Timur, known in the West as Tamburlaine, and Jenghis Khan. In 1526, leaving his capital, Kabul, Babur came down through the Hindu Kush on his fifth, and this time successful, raid into the sub-continent. He defeated the rulers of North India, the Lodis, at the Battle of Panipat, and then the confederacy of fierce Rajput rulers at the Battle of Khanua.

So began the Mughal Empire which flourished through six extraordinary rulers, the Great Mughals. Father to son, they ruled from 1526 until 1707, almost two centuries. With a mixture of military skill and enlightened patronage of the arts, they consolidated and expanded the Empire and brought it to unimaginable heights of power and splendour. At the death of the last Great Mughal, Aurangzeb, its vast territories stretched from Gujarat across to Bengal, from Kashmir right down almost to the tip of India. After them, the Empire began to wane. Weak Emperors followed one another to the throne only to be assassinated, deposed and blinded until the sunset of the once great power, when Bahadur Shah II was deposed by the British in 1858.

All six Emperors were great builders, but Shah Jahan was the greatest of all. He built the most buildings, and he built them the most lavishly and with the greatest taste and refinement. In all this, the inspiration of his lineage was as crucial as the ready-made and vastly wealthy empire he inherited.

For his brief reign, Babur (ruled 1526–30) took over the Lodis' capital, Agra. His building was restricted to laying out the first Mughal gardens in India, oases of lush flowers and trees criss-crossed by gurgling water-channels. These would be an important component of Shah Jahan's Red Fort. Humayun (ruled 1530–40 and 1555–6), his son, returned to the traditional power base of North India, Delhi, where he eventually died and was buried. Then came Akbar (ruled 1556–1605), perhaps the greatest Emperor of all, whose long reign roughly coincided with that of Elizabeth I of England. He was a soldier of genius and daring, an empire builder who turned a

A view from inside the Naqqar Khana back over the Chatta Chowk to the soaring Lahore Gate. By laying out a purpose-built city, Shah Jahan not only solved the problem of overcrowding at Agra, but also created a symmetrical stage-set for his ostentatious and thoroughly public Mughal Court ceremony, where each element of the scenery added to the performance of the players. Anyone arriving through this would be convinced he had reached the world's most magnificent Court.

foothold in India into control of the whole of Hindustan. Coming to the throne aged just thirteen, he expanded and strengthened the Empire with a winning combination of military flair, skilful diplomacy, religious tolerance and alliances sealed with marriage, especially with the fierce Rajput rulers. Akbar's achievements provided Shah Jahan, his grandson, with power and wealth, and his personality influenced the young prince.

Akbar's capital was back at Agra, where he built a magnificent, riverside fort with sturdy double walls. In 1571, aged just twenty-nine, he conceived and built his ideal city, Fatehpur Sikri, in thanks for the eventual birth of his first two sons. This personal dream palace-city of a young man was an instant artistic and intellectual centre; meanwhile, nearby Agra remained the military stronghold. Then, just as suddenly – perhaps because of lack of water, perhaps because Akbar had to make Lahore his base while securing the north-west frontier of his lands – it was abandoned in 1585. In the world's most perfect ghost-city, the red sandstone palace buildings are as crisp as when they were chiselled, and their rooms echo with court life, dancing, music, debate and processions.

Jahangir (ruled 1605–27) was the son of Akbar and his first Hindu wife, Jodhai Bai, daughter of the proud Rajput raja of Amber. Nurtured in the creative atmosphere of Fatehpur Sikri, he lifted Mughal Court culture to new levels of refinement, especially in painting and coins. He also built. At Agra, he completed Akbar's tomb and he aggrandized Akbar's palace by decorating it with polished and gold-painted stucco, and by adding more rooms and a striking façade with innovative white marble patterns set into the red sandstone.

Mughal luxury had arrived. Shah Jahan (ruled 1627–58) gladly refined it further. Already keen on architecture when he came to the throne, he soon began adding a string of palaces along the river front at Agra, using not sandstone but just the finest building material: pure white, gleaming marble. And for decoration he again used only the best: *pietra dura* inlay of precious and semi-precious stones to make delicate floral arabesques. The most exquisite work of all is in the Mussaman Burj, a mini-palace probably intended for his wife, Mumtaz Mahal, with courtyard, baths, living room and breeze-catching terrace.

The year 1631 was the tragic turning point for Shah Jahan. That year his beloved wife died. After two years of mourning, he threw himself into architecture with new frenzy, perhaps as consolation. First he built the perfect Mughal garden tomb for his wife, the Taj Mahal. Then, while adding the Moti Masjid (Pearl Mosque) at Agra and a new Diwan-i-Khas (Private Audience Hall) at Lahore, he took the boldest step of all: he decided to move the capital back to its traditional seat of power in North India, Delhi. In the style of previous Delhi rulers, he considered nothing existing there was good enough, so, in the grandest of all Mughal gestures, he laid out a fresh city, Shahjahanabad.

Perhaps the weight of his inheritance drove Shah Jahan to try to outshine his greatest forebears – Timur, Babur and Akbar. Certainly, with his considerable skill in architecture, building a city was an obvious way to glorify his name for posterity, especially if he could out-do Akbar's Fatehpur Sikri and Shah Abbas, creator of Persia's Isfahan. Inheriting an Empire that provided a continuous and mighty flow of income for the royal coffers, Shah Jahan could indulge his highly educated and refined eye in his greatest passion. Furthermore, the reduction of warfare in the stable Empire meant that the Court turned from being an itinerant camp into a more permanent lifestyle. New luxuries, time and space, led to an acceleration of pomp and show. And such ostentatious pageantry needed a stage. Agra offered no ceremonial axis, no processional route, and its narrow, twisting lanes were by now grossly overcrowded. Agra Fort was too small and, fuel to Shah Jahan's argument, some of its buildings were collapsing as a result of the Yamuna's lapping waters carving deep ravines into the walls. Lahore was little better. Purpose-built Shahjahanabad would be the answer to all his dreams.

The reasons for his choice of Delhi as his city's location were both political and religious. For centuries Delhi had been the irresistible capital for all rulers of North India, both Hindu and Muslim, because its strategic position made it the key to power in the sub-continent. It lay on the west bank of the Yamuna river, a tributary of the great Ganga, protected by a ring of hills on the otherwise flat and fertile plain. As political fortunes rose and fell, so successive conquerors each built a fresh stronghold, often choosing a virgin site and often naming it after himself. Thus Delhi has had eight major cities, energetic bursts of building by powerful overlords anxious to be remembered by posterity.

The Delhis began with Lal Kot, the Tomar Rajputs' citadel in the eighth to tenth centuries. Next came the Chauhan Rajputs, whose hero-king Prithviraj III built Qila Rai Pithora, the first Delhi to be named after its builder. In 1192, Prithviraj lost his city to the Turkish invader Qutb-ud-din Aibak, who proclaimed himself Sultan in 1206. Hindu rule ended and Muslim rule began, to continue until 1858. Aibak initiated the Delhi Sultanate (1206–1526), when successive Slave, Khalji, Tughluq, Sayyid and Lodi Sultans took their turns and the Muslim and Hindu cultures fused to create a rich Indo-Islamic society. Qutb-ud-din Aibak, the first Slave Sultan, merely added to the existing Delhi. Later Sultans built four fresh Delhis. Ala-ud-din Khalji, perhaps the ablest of all, built Siri in about 1303. The three Delhis of the Tughluq Sultans (ruled 1320–1413) followed: Tughluqabad, Jahanpanah and the greatest, Feroz Shah Kotla.

It was this impressive Tughluq city, thrown into instability after Sultan Feroz Shah's death in 1388, that caught the eye of Timur the Mongol, Babur's antecedant. In 1398, the army of the tough, stocky, sixty-year-old Timur sacked Delhi. As booty, they carried off to Samarkand not only much-prized Indian elephants and stonemasons but so much gold, jewels and other wealth that one eye-witness reported 'they could scarce march four miles a day' (in fact an exaggeration). Timur then sacked Lahore before crossing the Indus and returning home. He left behind him a carnage unprecedented in India's history. Just over a century later his descendant, Babur, returned and, instead of destruction, laid the seeds of the Mughal Empire which gave Muslim India its most sustained period of splendour.

But another Mughal Delhi came first, Purana Qila (Old Fort). Humayun, the second Mughal Emperor, founded it in 1533 as his Dinpanah (Shelter of the Faith). His are the two kilometres of soaring walls pierced by three giant, double-storey gateways, originally surrounded by a wide moat opening into the Yamuna. Like Shah Jahan after him, Humayun dreamt of a cultural capital to rival Samarkand. But Humayun, too self-indulgent and politically indecisive to consolidate the then fragile Mughal power, was ousted by Sher Shah Sur in 1540. It was not until 1555 that, with Sher Shah dead and his followers in a confusion, Humayun won Delhi back. The next year he died. The greatest monument of his time was his tomb, the most significant pre-Shah Jahan Mughal building in Delhi. Built by his senior widow, Bega

Above, afternoon sunlight glows on the three rows of red sandstone columns supporting the cusped arches and roof of the Diwan-i-Am pavilion. This, the goal of all his subjects and visitors, was where Shah Jahan held his daily public audiences with tremendous aplomb and all the panoply of a theatrical impressario.

Below, the Diwan-i-Khas was the Emperor's private audience hall, a riverside palace reserved for ministers and high-ranking, favoured visitors. Here Shah Jahan sat on his Peacock Throne at the centre of his Fort, cooled by riverside breezes wafting through the floor-level windows, soft light reflecting off the gilded ceilings and walls, fine silk rugs strewn on the marble floor.

The Diwan-i-Khas, the most richly decorated of all the Red Fort buildings, was Shah Jahan's private audience hall for the equivalent of his cabinet meetings. Its decoration is the apogee of Mughal taste, a carefully balanced combination of opulence, extravagance and refinement. In this corner, various elaborately decorated elements exist happily together. The marble piers and scalloped arches are carved and painted with cartouches and bold floral arabesques. They rise to meet two broad borders painted on contrasting grounds of white and gold which act as frames for the carved and painted lattice-work of the wooden ceiling.

A closer look at Shah Jahan's built-in throne in the Diwan-i-Am reveals a riot of refined, top quality pietra dura inlay work, denser even than in the Mussaman Burg at Agra Fort. Here the lily designs of the baldichin canopy contrast with the bolder bird panels of the back wall.

Above, the worldwide legend of the Red Fort attracted tourists from the moment it was built, and continues to do so. Here, a few of the eight to ten thousand daily visitors to the Red Fort peep into the Hammams, the royal baths, which are currently closed to the public.

Below, and this is what the visitor sees through the window: a bathroom of unbelievable luxury, surviving proof that every detail of Shah Jahan's Fort originally lived up to the legendary high standards of Mughal taste and craftsmanship. The floor is a carpet of marble with pietra dura *inlay, while the faceted ceiling is the perfect foil to its richness.*

Begum, and designed by a Persian, Mirak Mirza Ghiyas, this is the first Mughal garden tomb and the first great Indo-Islamic Mughal building.

Religious tradition was also significant to the choice of the site. Delhi was, for Muslims, a major pilgrimage centre. Here was the dargah (shrine) of the Sufi saint Shaikh Nizamu'd-Din Auliya Chishti (1236–1325), right at the heart of Nizamuddin village, near Purana Qila. The court poet and saint, Amir Khusrau (died 1325) was also buried here (one of his couplets would be inscribed on Shah Jahan's palace walls in the Red Fort). The tombs of other Muslim holy men are nearby.

The Sufi saint acquired a string of royal devotees including two Tughluq Sultans and several Mughal Emperors. When Babur was in Delhi in 1526 he visited the shrine. Humayun, as we have seen, was buried close by. According to the official diary, the Akbarnama, it was during Akbar's visit there in 1576 that the arrow of an assassin 'struck His Majesty's right shoulder' but failed to kill him 'as the Divine protection and the prayers of the saints were guarding him'. Shah Jahan himself visited the Sufi saint's tomb in 1633 when he returned from the Deccan. And his daughter Jahanara, who laid out Chandni Chowk in Shahjahanabad, was buried here. Indeed, Delhi became known to Muslims as 'Hazrat [revered] Delhi . . . the guardian of religion and justice'.

This, then, was the background to Shah Jahan's decision to uproot the vast administrative bandwagon of the Mughal Empire and trundle it back to Delhi. These were the 'promptings of his generous heart'. For a powerful, stable ruler who wanted to build a great city, Delhi was the obvious choice. And while other Mughal cities are now dead, and all previous Delhis are reduced to picturesque ruins, Shah Jahan's lives on and the kernal of his Red Fort still stands.

The Man, the Dream, the Reality

1

'Shah Jahan was a man of great executive ability, to which he added a love for the magnificent and a refined artistic sense, specially for architecture. He was in a special sense the architectural director of his day and there seems to be little doubt that the great buildings of his reign . . . would not have been what they are without his personal inspiration and direction. As a ruler he governed India firmly for thirty years and left behind him a legend of magnificence, rough justice, and prosperity.' Percival Spear, *A History of India*, 1978.

This is just one side of the personality of the fifth Mughal Emperor. Other characteristics were, as Spear points out, less attractive. For here was a ruthless man, who at his succession executed all the male Mughal collaterals, even though at the time they were of little political significance. He loved his wife dearly, but did not hesitate to expose her to the rigours of constant military campaigns (a punishing schedule even by nomadic Mughal standards) and to the endurance of fourteen pregnancies, the last one finally killing her at the age of thirty-nine. In later life he became so hedonistic that even in an atmosphere tolerant of such behaviour, his was remarked upon. In brief, Shah Jahan gained power by ruthlessness and lost it to his third son, Aurangzeb, through self-indulgence, ending his days a pathetic prisoner in Agra Fort, gazing across the waters to his wife's tomb, the Taj Mahal.

Shahab-ud-din Muhammad Sahib Qiran Sani Shah Jahan ascended the Mughal throne in Agra in 1627, aged thirty-five. In 1639 he decided to move the capital to Delhi. On 29 April, he watched the foundation-stone being laid, and nine years later, on 8 April, 1648, the sparkling new Fort and city were inaugurated. It takes a remarkable person to create a large, thriving capital city that is an immediate success and lives on, seemingly, in perpetuity.

Shah Jahan's preparation for the throne began early. He was born Prince Khurram in Lahore on 5 January, 1592. Although his lineage was three-quarters Hindu, the Prince was to have little Hindu influence in his life; he did not marry any Hindus and failed to promote the religious tolerance his grandfather, Akbar, had displayed. On the contrary, he grew up to become an ardent Muslim, more orthodox than his father, Jahangir (whose own mother was a Hindu), but more pragmatic than his successor, Aurangzeb. Nevertheless, it was his grandfather who played a large part

Emperor Shah Jahan, builder and patron of the arts, is shown here seated in the jewel-encrusted Peacock Throne he commissioned. The jewel merchant Jean Baptist Tavernier declared it to be 'the principal [of] seven magnificent thrones, one wholly covered with diamonds, the others with rubies, emeralds, or pearls.' Whereas this painting, an eighteenth-century watercolour copy of an earlier version, gives the throne a pair of peacocks, the more trustworthy Tavernier described only one.

in his childhood – indeed, the little boy grew to be his grandfather's favourite choice for the throne, over and above his father and older brothers. Khurram was the youngest son, and so was invariably the centre of affection, and it is said that royal astrologers were quick to begin concocting a horoscope predicting his destiny as Emperor. It was Akbar who planned Khurram's early education, promoting his royal future in the knowledge that it took an unorthodox Muslim to rule successfully over a large Hindu majority. Meanwhile, he was trained in Mughal court etiquette by the governess of Akbar's cousin, Ruqiah Sultan Begum.

Following Mughal tradition, Khurram's formal education began at the age of four years, four months and four days. Akbar chose his first teacher, Mulla Qasim Beg, a considerable Sufi scholar, whose team taught the budding Prince archery, fencing, shooting, riding and wrestling. This was typical of Akbar, who had stoically refused to learn to read and write, excelled at sport and remained illiterate all his life – his education was tactfully described by Abu'l Fazl, his recorder, as carrying off 'the ball of excellence with the polo stick of divine help'. But such an education was not to Khurram's father's satisfaction. He switched his tutors, employing Hakim Ali Gillani, whose more orthodox approach instilled languages, sciences and a sense of discipline. Fortunately, Khurram's intelligence, common sense and accute observation responded.

Undaunted, Akbar took his six-year-old grandson off on a military expedition in 1598. It was quite tough: an eighty-three day march to Agra, with stops for camping, hunting and Akbar's religious debates. The next year they both went right down to the Deccan, returning in 1601. Khurram saw the real life of a military camp, attended meetings when military strategies were planned, and was taught the forbidden riding, shooting and swordmanship. Hakim Ali accompanied them, so warfare was mixed with mathematics, religion and philosophy.

Because of their close relationship, Akbar's death in 1605 hit the young boy hard. Clearly the old Emperor had wanted his son to be passed over in favour of one of his grandsons. For his son Salim, whose birth in 1569 encouraged Akbar to build Fatehpur Sikri, his ideal city near Agra, had become debauched and unreliable during his long wait for the throne, aided by drink and opium (his two younger brothers had already died of drink). Akbar openly began to favour Salim's oldest son,

Above, the red sandstone façade of the Diwan-i-Am. When Shah Jahan held his daily public audiences here, the columns and ceilings were painted and gilded, and brightly coloured awnings hung from the iron rings, which are still in place.

Below, as the sun lifts, the faithful of Shahjahanbad pause on the northern steps of Shah Jahan's great Jama Masjid, used by him when he lived in the Red Fort. The arcades enclosing the great courtyard are up on the plinth behind them.

A close look at one pair of capitals in the Diwan-i-Am reveals both the high standard of carving and the high quality of the Fatehpur Sikri sandstone, which has hardly worn over more than three centuries. To reach this standard throughout the Fort, a huge and highly skilled workforce was recruited.

Khusrau – whatever his affections for Khurram, the third son, the first-born was next in line. In September 1605 he staged an elephant fight between Salim and Khusrau's strongest elephants, hoping to find an omen for the future. The old Emperor watched from his pavilion with Khurram sitting at his side. Salim's elephant won. When both camps began fighting, Akbar sent thirteen-year-old Khurram down to rebuke his father and brother. A month later Akbar died and Salim became a far better Emperor than Akbar had expected.

Salim chose the name Jahangir (Seizer of the World). Coming to the throne at the age of thirty-six, he ruled for twenty-two years before asthma banished him to the solace and gentle climate of his Kashmir gardens for the last time. At the beginning of his reign, his young son Khurram shone in military campaigns in Rajasthan and then in the Deccan, where his successful negotiations encouraged his father to reward him at Mandu with a magnificent feast, the honour of sitting in his father's presence and the title of Shah Jahan (Ruler of the World), which he used when he became Emperor.

Sir Thomas Roe (in India 1615–19) witnessed the whole event somewhat contemptuously. An envoy from James I who scampered after Jahangir trying to discuss trade deals, Roe was later regarded as Britain's first unofficial ambassador to India. Roe had already seen Khurram at close quarters when he was Governor of Gujarat and given this candid view of the mature, twenty-four-year-old prince: 'I never saw so settled a countenance, nor any man keepe so constant a gravity, never smiling, nor in face showing any respect or difference of men; but mingled with extreme pride and contempt of all. Yet I found some inward trouble now and then assayle him, and a kind of brokennes and distraction in his thoughts, uprovidedly and amasedly answering sutors, or not hearing.'

A ruthless determination to shine lay behind this cold façade, of which the most influential person at Court took full note. This was Nur Jahan, Jahangir's wife. First she supported him while he excelled on the battlefield; then, seeing there would be no place for her in his Court, she turned against him. Pushed aside, Khurram drifted into rebellion, and soon murdered his brother Khusrau. The next brother, Parviz, drunk himself to death. At Jahangir's death, Shah Jahan coolly ordered the murder of his younger brother, Shahriyar, plus two nephews and two cousins. His throne was secure.

Shah Jahan's reign began happily. When not on campaign, he lived in style and security at Agra, beginning his palace improvements. His Queen, Arjumand Banu, whom he had first met at a royal bazaar in the Fort, took the name Mumtaz Mahal (Chosen one of the Palace). Unlike the dominant Nur Jahan, she was a constant companion and valued adviser to her husband, but tragedy struck in June 1631 when she died in the Deccan giving birth to their fourteenth child. Shah Jahan was heartbroken. He mourned for two years, giving up music, feasting and glamorous garments. Then, putting his campaigns into the hands of his sons – a move that proved foolhardy in the long run – he threw his energy into building.

During his military campaigns, the observant prince had already noted the full variety of architecture in the sub-continent, although his passion to see Samarkand and Isfahan – perhaps inspirations for Shahjahanabad – was never fulfilled: he never left his Empire. As well as appreciating buildings he saw and receiving detailed reports of cities he heard about, his practical experience of architecture began early. As a youth, Khurram went on expedition to Kabul, where the palaces, forts, gardens and historic atmosphere gave him a clear understanding of the origins of the Mughal dynasty. Here, aged fifteen, he remodelled a mansion in one of Babur's favourite gardens, Pratap Bagh. Even his father was impressed: 'Gifted with a high sense of archæological excellence, Khurram ordered and supervised alterations required to be carried out and made the house his headquarters for the entire duration of his stay.'

More ambitious building soon followed. Still as a young man, Khurram added a mosque to the Mughal's most sacred shrine, the Dargah Sharif (Holy Shrine) of the Sufi saint Khwaja Muin-ud-din Chishti at Ajmer in Rajasthan. A hundred feet long, with eleven arches along the front, it already set the tone for later buildings; and it was Shah Jahan's first building in marble. Near here, he also built the three marble arches on the banks of Ana Sagar, a man-made lake. While Governor of Gujarat, he added a sarai (inn) and palace to the already splendid city of Ahmedabad. While Governor of the Deccan, he saw the fine sultanate cities and attended his father's Court at Mandu, like Ahmedabad a city full of magnificent buildings.

In 1619, now twenty-seven years old, Khurram travelled with his father to Kashmir,

This bird's-eye view from the river (east) side of the Fort was painted, with a little artistic licence, in Lucknow in 1780–90 by a Company School artist. It shows an emperor, probably Shah Alam (ruled 1759–1806), walking from his Khas Mahal to the Diwan-i-Khas. What is especially clear are the east-west axis and courtyard layout of the whole Fort. The Diwan-i-Khas and Rang Mahal courtyards have blue curtains across their entrances (although contemporary diarists record them as being red) and, further back, a great blue awning shades the inner area of the Diwan-i-Am courtyard. Behind that, beyond the Naqqar Khana, Chatta Chowk stretches westwards to Lahore Gate, while more bazaars line the wide north-south parade. The harem fills the left (south) side of the painting, while Aurangzeb's Moti Masjid is just visible on the right. (British Library, London)

where he was entrusted with much of the design and supervision of Jahangir's Shalimar Gardens at Srinagar: the red sandstone boundary wall with alcoves and pavilions have the Shah Jahan stamp. (He would later lay out his own eighty-acre Shalimar Gardens at Lahore, in 1637.) Then, as a less contented rebel Prince from around 1622 onwards, he travelled the length and breadth of India until Jahangir's death in 1627.

Thus Shah Jahan saw and absorbed by the finest buildings of India. Throughout his travels, he displayed an intense and sophisticated interest in architecture which helped him acquire the highly developed sense of æsthetics reflected in his own buildings. His early works show how keen he himself was to build, and display a genuine talent which is a foretaste of that displayed in his grand projects.

From the time of his accession to the throne, Shah Jahan's sense of æsthetics needs to be seen in the context of the Emperor's view on other subjects. For instance, he adored the pomp and show of Court, and his insatiable zest for life could be satisfied only by constant pleasure and pageantry. In addition to building, he patronized all the fine arts, nursing a special passion for planting symmetrical gardens of stone, trees, grass and water. And it is said he considered music 'the only sensual pleasure without vice'.

Shah Jahan's administrative strength was in his orderliness, and, immune to flatterers, he improved his finances by better management, by sacking bad bureaucrats and by cutting down on unnecessary administrative expenditure. Much of this extra money would be poured into his building projects – Shah Jahan's income was said to be twice that of Akbar, while he spent three times as much. His building mania ensured that the imperial exchequer would never again be able to bear the strain of such extravagance.

Shah Jahan's religious views are relevant to his architectural taste, too. He had no sympathy with the tolerance of Akbar or the looseness of Jahangir's Court. His attitude to Islam was straightforward and orthodox, which influenced his conscious return to Muslim culture, clearly seen in the more Persian qualities of his building. Although he was not as extreme as his successor, Aurangzeb, he abolished ceremonial protestation before the throne, which smacked too much of divine worship. But his actions became more extreme after his wife Mumtaz's death. In 1632, his troops burned down a Portuguese Jesuit settlement at Hooghly, and in 1633 he ordered the demolition of Hindu temples at Varanasi and prohibited the erection of new Hindu shrines or the restoration of old ones. In 1634 he forbade mixed marriages between Hindus and Muslims; and he positively encouraged mass conversions of Hindus to Islam.

As soon as he was in power, Shah Jahan began building, focusing on his two fort-palaces at Lahore and Agra. His was to be, in Percy Brown's words, 'the reign of marble', when the Mughal golden age 'found expression in a style of architecture of exceptional splendour . . . carried out to the highest degree of perfection'. The smooth polish, the costly luxury and the brilliant whiteness of marble so perfectly fitted Shah Jahan's taste that not only did he build in it whenever possible, but he actively tore down some rough red sandstone buildings and replaced them with marble ones. This he did at both Lahore and Agra, which were connected, via Delhi, by the Grand Trunk Road built by Sher Shah Sur and given a new, 400-mile avenue of shade-giving trees by Shah Jahan. Lahore Fort had been built by Akbar and improved by Jahangir, who added the remarkable glazed picture gallery on the exterior wall. The year he became Emperor, Shah Jahan demolished Akbar's sandstone structures along the northern side and began to replace them with a marble Diwan-i-Am (Public Audience Hall), Khwab Garh, Shish Mahal (Mirror Palace), Musamman Burj (Octagonal Tower) and Naulakha.

Agra Fort, his principal home at this period, received similar but more devoted treatment over the next decade. It was to be the practice run for the Red Fort at Delhi. Agra had been Akbar's most magnificent fort, his carved palace rooms overlooking the Yamuna waters which lapped against the protective double walls. Jahangir made additions, but Shah Jahan again tore down sandstone, replacing some of the riverside royal apartments with a string of exquisite, chaste, marble creations. The five-arched Khas Mahal (Private Palace) is at the south end, which Shah Jahan called his Aramgah (Place of Rest). It is flanked by two pavilions for his two favourite daughters, Jahanara and Roshanara: roofs were curved and elongated, marble riverside screens filtered in light but kept out heat, and the air was cooled with playing fountains. To the royal Hammams (baths) he added two antechambers known as the Shish Mahal, as their ceilings were set with glass which twinkled in

Muslims make use of Aurangzeb's private and tiny Moti Masjid. Although perhaps a more devout Muslim than his predecessors, Shah Jahan made no provision for a mosque inside the Red Fort walls and was content to use the great congregational Jama Masjid in the city centre. Indeed, although it was not begun until 1650, the Jama Masjid was vital to the original concept that the Fort and city should interrelate.

When Aurangzeb added his mosque, the Moti Masjid, he was continuing his father's predeliction for white marble, but less ostentatiously. The marble-coated onion domes, delicate inlaid frieze and slender minarets give a clue to the richness lying behind the anonymous red sandstone walls. Aurangzeb placed his mosque behind the Hammams, beside the gardens at the north end of the private palace area. Thus it was both convenient to his Diwan-i-Khas and Khas Mahal, while causing the least disturbance to Shah Jahan's carefully laid out palace buildings and courtyards.

Above, although both are built of royal stone, marble, and extravagantly decorated, the Khas Mahal which the widower Shah Jahan built in the Red Fort has a fierce exterior anonymity and a demand for privacy absent from the open and welcoming suite of rooms he built for himself and his family at Agra.

Below, with the shifting sands of the Yamuna River, what was selected by the builders of the Red Fort as a prime site with river protection and river breezes on the east is today a dry, grassy waste – the river has moved several hundred yards away. But, ever entrepreneurial, the locals congregate here on Sunday mornings and hold a flea-market. With plenty of space, the dhurrie-seller is able to sit huddled in his grey shawl having laid out all his colourful merchandise for a potential client.

the candelight – a trick used more extensively at Delhi. But the cluster of buildings that reveals the maturity and refinement of Shah Jahan's aesthetics is Mussaman Burj. Its perfectly proportioned and gloriously inlaid chambers form a self-contained, all marble mini-palace with courtyard, baths, living room and breeze-catching terrace. Probably built for Mumtaz, this is where Shah Jahan lived out the last nine years of his life. Above this is the equally ravishing Diwan-i-Khas, built in 1637, its double columns some of the most graceful Shah Jahan built.

It was Shah Jahan's devotion to marble that most influenced the architectural changes. The stone came from Makrana, near Jaipur, and dictated the newly smooth, uncluttered lines, responding well to an emphasis on structural shape. The nine-cusped arch became a favourite device, which stands out as a silhouette best when built in white marble; and arcades of cusped arches are characteristic of Shah Jahan's building. Marble also dictated the decoration, as its smooth lines need only the most restrained mouldings. Where decoration was added, it was with inlay rather than fancy carving, and it was usually in the form of delicate floral arabesques or vases of flowers, made of precious and semi-precious stones. Above all, the classic simplicity of a marble building is shown off to greatest advantage when it is just a single room deep and seen not in a cluster but isolated, if possible on a raised platform in a controlled environment such as an enclosed courtyard. In essence, it makes perfect stage scenery – as Shah Jahan was to demonstrate in the Red Fort.

Marble also showed off to best advantage Shah Jahan's return to the more Persian form of dome, with bulbous outline and narrow neck. In Agra Fort he added two marble mosques, the tiny Nagina Masjid built for his ladies, and the Moti Masjid, one of his finest single buildings. Begun after he had started work on Shahjahanabad, it is remarkable not only for its proportions, for the rhythm of its colonnaded cloisters and for the brilliant use of material, but above all for the subtle way the central dome rises on its drum, seemingly weightlessly.

This lightness pervades Shah Jahan's best-known building, the Taj Mahal. Two years after Mumtaz died, he concentrated his despair into creating her mausoleum. An estimated 20,000 labourers and craftsmen contributed their skills, some travelling from Europe, and twenty-one years later it was complete. It takes to ultimate refinement the Mughal garden tomb first seen in Humayun's tomb at Delhi, but here the proportions are more satisfying, the inlay work more refined and the building material is pure white marble. The outer gates lead to a single inner one, which forces every visitor to have his first view of the Taj head on. It stands on a platform silhouetted against the harsh blue Indian sky, its marble glowing with additional reflected light from the Yamuna. Surely Shah Jahan was remembering its effect when he was designing the layout of the Red Fort.

With the building of the Taj under way and Agra and Lahore palace-forts improved as much as possible, Shah Jahan turned his attention to his most ambitious building project: a new capital city, necessary because both Agra and Lahore had tiny, cluttered lanes quite unsuitable for his lifestyle and his now vast Court retinue. First, a site had to be chosen. Under the guidance of Shah Jahan's Mir-i-Imarat (Supervisor of Buildings), the architects, engineers and the all-important astrologers were sent to look for a beautiful spot where the new capital would shine as a symbol of power and wealth. Mughals believed the capital to be the *axis mundi*, the centre of the earth, where the celestial and mundane worlds met. Delhi was the obvious choice as the traditional seat of power and a major sacred pilgrimage centre for Muslims (the late seventeenth-century historian, Sujan Rai, wrote that 'there are so many saints' tombs . . . that their number can't be expressed in writing'). After various suggestions, including one spot near Nizamuddin, the exact site selected was north of all the previous cities (except the small citadel of Salimgarh), a bluff overlooking the Yamuna river.

Next came the concept. The city's prime function was to be a stage set for a non-stop show exalting Shah Jahan as the richest and most powerful Emperor in the world. It followed the pattern of a palace-fortress, divided into two parts, special and ordinary. The Red Fort was the special part, the seat of power accessible only to those who were part of that power, and had its own wall. The city was the ordinary part, where less important business was conducted and where lesser members of the royal household, such as princes and amirs (commanders), lived and ran the various areas. Its focus was the great mosque, the Jama Masjid, to which the Emperor would ride every Friday. Thus Fort and city were interdependent.

Then came the precise plan, designed by Ustad Ahmed Lahori. This seems to combine both Persian and Hindu thought. Persian is evident in the formal geometric

Above, Shah Jahan repaired the Nahr-i Bihisht canal to ensure a reliable supply of water into his capital. It entered the Red Fort at Shah Burj, behind this magnificent marble cascade and canopy later added by Aurangzeb. The water would tinkle over the patterned cascade down into the shell-shaped pool, dancing a reflection on the pietra dura inlay decorating the back wall. It then made its way southwards, towards the Hammams and palaces.

Below, the cooling waters of the Nahr-i Bihisht flowed through the Khas Mahal, seen in the distance, across the blinding heat of the courtyard and into the Rang Mahal where they reached this superb marble fountain, originally inlaid with stones whose colours danced up through the waters and were reflected in the lavish wall and ceiling decoration. To the left, a canal took some water to fall over a cascade of marble niches and into a garden pool.

Above, Shah Jahan's preparation for this Emperor's-eye view began when he was a young boy. This is taken from his throne in the Diwan-i-Am, where he would have looked out over his ministers, then his lesser ministers, then the great crowd of subjects filling the courtyard and pouring in through the Naqqar Khana. When someone especially important arrived, such as an ambassador, he was heralded by musicians playing up above. However, François Bernier noted that 'persons of all ranks, high and low, rich and poor' came, 'because it is in this extensive hall that the King gives audience indiscriminately to all his subjects'.

Below, the first job was to build the defences for the city and, inside, the citadel-fort. Twenty-one towers and seven main gateways punctuated the 4 mile long, 27 foot high city wall. The walls encircling the 124 acre Fort were even more tremendous, ranging in height from 60 feet on the river side to 75 on the landward side, and in width from 45 feet at ground level to 30 feet at the top. This section shows one of the Fort's 21 towers (7 round and 14 octagonal) built into the wall, in addition to the 4 main gates and 2 minor ones.

layout, with symmetrical gardens, palaces and avenues, and the architectural forms of the palace buildings – although Hindu stonemasons and craftsmen ensured some Hindu elements. Hindu is the inspiration for the whole shape of the city, like a curved bow (facing the river) with the most important building, the Red Fort, at the intersection of the bow and arm, and for the notion of dividing the city into different neighbourhoods. However, both ideas, from the ancient *Silpa sastras* (Rules for manual arts), were a regular part of Indian town planning by the seventeenth century, and therefore no longer consciously Hindu.

The layout made full use of the site's potential. The Red Fort was on the bluff and beside the river, both natural defences; and riverside palaces got the best of the cool, unpolluted east breezes. Close members of the royal family had mansions to north and south – Dara Shukoh near Kashmir Gate, for instance, and Akbarabadi Begum in Daryaganj area. The only prominent hillock, Bhujalal Pahari (Bhujalal Hill), was reserved for the capital's principal mosque, the Jama Masjid. Ingenious planning ensured a royal route to it and careful patronage ensured that favourite and loyal courtiers lived along the route.

The palaces and mosque were the two focuses, and the rest of the Red Fort and city were laid out around them. Within the Fort, the east-west axis led from the Diwan-i-Am through the Naqqar Khana (Drum House) and the covered Chatta Chowk out through Lahore Gate. Straight ahead lay the long, wide Chandni Chowk, the city's main bazaar and axis, lined with shops and elegant palaces, mosques and gardens. Behind them, the mud and thatched homes of the rest of the population were clustered in a maze of often yard-wide lanes, each area called a mohallah and devoted to a particular craft or profession, which often holds true today – Dariba Kalan for jewellers, others for spices, oil, leather, sugar, milk, and so on. Two more wide avenues led from the Fort's Delhi Gate, Faiz Bazar southwards and Khas Bazar south-westwards to the Jama Masjid. North of Chandni Chowk were the city's public facilities, its gardens, sarais (inns), ghats (river steps) and Hammams (baths); south of it lived most of the population, with the Jama Masjid in the centre. The whole city was encircled by a great protective stone wall.

With the basic plan fixed, Shah Jahan was eager to start work. On 29 April, 1639, an auspicious day selected by the royal astrologers, Ghairat Kahn, Governor of Delhi, ordered the two builders Ustad Hira and Ustad Hamid to begin excavating (the lanes where they lived are still named after them). 'The foundations were marked out with the usual ceremonies,' wrote Muhammad Tahir in the *Shahjahan-nama* in 1657–58, 'according to the plan devised, in the august presence . . . and the foundation-stone of that noble structure was laid.' And, to ensure the success of the project, Shah Jahan tossed the bodies of several newly beheaded criminals into the trenches as a sacrifice. In a miraculous two weeks, the foundations were ready.

The power of the Emperor was instrumental in gathering the vast workforce needed, for, as Muhammad Tahir continued, 'throughout the Imperial dominions, wherever artificers could be found . . . by the mandate worthy of implicit obedience, they were all collected together, and multitudes of common labourers were employed in the work'. A huge contingent arrived, including builders, carpenters and stonemasons, 'skilled in both plain and decorative work'. Red sandstone was brought by river and land (causing great traffic jams) from the Fatehpur Sikri quarries, marble from Makrana. Niccolao Manucci (in India 1656–1717), an Italian solider and quack doctor whose gossip-filled diary about his Indian travels was a best-seller in Europe, also noted that Shah Jahan was not above plundering past Delhis for materials, for 'he used the ruins of ancient Dihli and Toquilabad [Tugh-laqabad] for building his new Dihli'. Feaverish work began on the Red Fort; in the city, nobles were awarded plots of land for their mansions and began building, too. Nine years later the city was complete.

It was a vast achievement, not without the odd mishap. The stone, brick and lime city wall was 3.8 miles long, 27 feet high and 12 feet thick, topped by 27 towers and pierced by 7 major gates for roads and 3 for reaching the river ghats. The gates were Kashmiri, Mori, Kabuli, Lahori, Ajmeri, Turkomani and Akbarabadi; the ghats were Raj, Qila and Nigambodh. The city wall alone took seven years to build, after the first hasty attempt using stone and mud had collapsed in monsoon rains. Inside the walls, the Red Fort covered 124 acres and had its own wall. Chandni Chowk, the city's largest and richest bazaar, was built in 1650 by Shah Jahan's favourite daughter, Jahanara. It was 1,520 yards long, 40 yards wide, lined with mansions and 1,560 shops (each a single room with a warehouse behind and living space above) and cooled by the central Nahr-i Bihisht (Canal of Paradise). The next largest was

Left, here, in the Diwan-i-Am, the use of strong Fatehpur Sikri sandstone has meant that the leaves of the pilaster capital are as crisp as when they were carved. The hard, non-porous – and so non-staining – white marble comes from Makrana, near Jaipur, whose quarries produced the marble for the Taj Mahal. And the polished limestones, marbles and semi-precious stones for the pietra dura heron and his companions came from all over north India and even further afield.

Right, this detail of the arch between Shah Jahan's throne and the back wall of the Diwan-i-Am reveals the precision workmanship for which Indian craftsmen are still known. First, the pieces of white marble are cut and prepared. While the lattice-work is being carved, a workshop of pietra dura craftsmen decorate each flat piece of marble. For each piece, the marble is coated with red water-based paint and the paper design pricked through. Stones are then selected for their colour and clarity – the orange-red petals of these flowers are cornelian which varies in quality from a fine, firey red to the less good banded pink. Then the slow work of cutting each stone and chiselling a bed for it begins, usually preparing the big flowers first, then the leaves and lastly the stems. Each stone is cut, fitted, fine-tuned with an emery paste wheel and then glued and heated to fuse the stone. When the design is complete, the whole surface is polished with increasingly fine emery.

Gardens were an integral and essential part of Mughal life. Babur, newly arrived from Persia, bemoaned their absence and considered 'one of the chief defects of Hindustan is the want of artificial water-courses'. Shah Jahan made two large gardens and several smaller ones part of the Red Fort plan, their water-courses, such as this one, fed by the Nahr-i Bihisht canal.

Faiz Bazar (Bazaar of Plenty), built the same year by one of Shah Jahan's several senior wives, Nawab Akbarabadi Begum, with 888 shops in its 1,050 yards.

Plans for bringing in essential, life-giving water (the lack of which had probably forced Akbar to leave his Fatehpur Sikri) represent one of the most impressive engineering feats of the whole Mughal period. Indeed, its watercourses were one of the main reasons for Shahjahanabad's reputation as city of greenness and beauty. The Nahr-i Bihisht canal ran from the Yamuna at a point 75 miles upstream and followed a very circuitous route. Firoz Shah Tughluq is said to have begun it around 1355; Akbar had repaired and extended it, and in 1639 Shah Jahan did the same. His engineer Ali Mardan Khan added another 78 miles to its length, plus a five-arch aqueduct. As it passed through the outskirts of Shahjahanabad, it was 25 feet wide and deep, and provided water for gardens and homes before entering the city by the Kabuli Gate. It then split into two main branches, one serving the two great bazaars, the other watering Jahanara's 50-acre garden, Sahibabad (Abode of the Master). It then continued to the north-eastern corner of the Red Fort. Here, beside the Shah Burj (King's Tower), a device called a *shutrgulu* (camel's neck) lifted the water up to the palace level so it could gurgle its way through the palace chambers and the royal gardens. In all, the canal, observed Sujan Rai, 'confers freshness on the gardens in the suburbs ... lends happiness to the streets and bazars, and enhances the splendour of the imperial palaces.'

Building the city must have been an administrative nightmare. Three governors of Delhi oversaw it: Ghairat Khan was first, but when the foundations were begun and some of the materials gathered, he was replaced by Ilahawardi Khan. He lasted two years, while the Red Fort walls went up, but it was Mukramat Khan who controlled the bulk of the building operations. The chronicler Samsan-ud-Daula, writing in 1747, later gave him due credit: 'As a result of his unstinted efforts this huge fort with its heavenly appurtenances was completed in the 20th year [of Shah Jahan's reign]. It had on all corners heavenly palaces, and at every angle gardens and parks.' But above all, it was the Emperor's 'personal inspiration and direction' which brought together the creative energies, skills, labour force, materials and dedication needed to build Shahjahanabad, the City of Shah Jahan, with its magnificent Red Fort.

The Emperor in his Fort

2

'There is one place in Delhi, the first sight of which is surely unforgettable. It is enshrined behind the Titanic rose-pink walls of the vast Fort, those huge masses that look as though they were built for all time. You would never dream that such grim portals could conceal a retreat so enchanting. The great battlements tower above you as you enter a formidable gateway, and stand wondering in the centre of a gigantic hall with vaulted roof. It is like the nave of a cathedral. Beyond it, you enter an open space that is called a courtyard but is the size of a London square. You cross it, advance through another mighty archway and confront the Diwan-i-Am.' Lovat Fraser, *At Delhi*, 1903.

On 19 April, 1648, another auspicious day selected by the royal astrologers, Shah Jahan entered his new city amid jubilant celebrations which lasted for ten days. The triumphant life of Shahjahanabad began. The whole of the Red Fort was decked in splendour. It was already dubbed Qila-i-Mualla (Exalted Fort) by some, and Qila Mubarak (Auspicious Fort) by the ever-tactful court historians; today it is known as Lal Qila (Red Fort). Writers eulogized over it, with constant references to paradise and the heavens. According to Samsam-ud-Daula, writing a century later, the royal apartments were strewn with carpets 'prepared in Kashmir and Lahore out of selected wool with great skill and taste . . . [and] in every apartment were placed jewelled, gold enamelled and plainly worked thrones', whose cushions 'with brilliant pearls' rested on 'gold embroidered cloths'. Indeed, every surface of the audience halls and the porticoes of all the other rooms 'were covered up and decorated with embroidered canopies, golden curtains from Europe and China, gold and silver embroidered velvets from Gujarat and gold and silver-thread screens'.

When the moment came, Shah Jahan entered his city by the river gate on the east side and went first to his Diwan-i-Khas (Private Audience Hall) around which his wazir (superintendent), Saadullah Khan, had created a silver enclosure. There was also a grander, golden enclosure whose alcoves were hung with 'golden stars with golden chains' which 'made the place resemble the heavens'. The Peacock Throne was in the middle, beneath a pearl and gold-embroidered canopy 'raised on jewelled poles' and flanked by pearl-encrustred parasols. Behind here were displayed the Qur Khana (Royal Armoury), whose bejewelled swords, scabbards, quivers and spears

When Shah Jahan made his triumphal entry into his Red Fort on April 19, 1648, he first came to his Diwan-i-Khas, which had been splendidly decked out for the occasion. Running down the centre of this and the other private riverside palaces were the cooling waters of the Nahr-i Bihisht canal, most welcome as April is already a hot month in Delhi. Here in the Diwan-i-Khas, the marble floor covers the canal to enable high-ranking ministers to approach the Emperor's throne which stood in front of the riverside window on the left. Beyond the Diwan-i-Khas, the canal reaches Khas Mahal, whose central room is given extra privacy with a marble screen.

Right, Shah Jahan entered his sparkling new city through the river gateway at the bottom of Mussaman Burj, the domed octagonal tower of his private quarters, Khas Mahal. This entry, reserved for him and for great statesmen, emerged at ground level in the courtyard on the far side. The tower is the only room to jut forward and break the smooth line of the Fort wall. This is where the people gathered on the river banks to witness the Emperor performing his first public duty of the day by showing himself, safe and sound, to his subjects at the Jharokah-i Darshan, the Showing Balcony — although he probably looked through a window, for the little balcony is a later addition.

Below, the Lahore Gate was, and still is, the principal entrance to the Fort. Rising high above the walls and with the Indian tricolour flying above, the full view of its majesty is now blocked by Aurangzeb's barbican. In Shah Jahan's time, horses were exercised here in the early morning, and travellers, merchants and ambassadors arrived here to try to gain entry to the world's most dazzling Court. Later, even without the splendid Mughal trappings, the nineteenth-century poet and traveller Wilfred Scawen Blunt wrote in his secret diary: 'The mosque is far and away the finest mosque, the palace far and away the finest palace; and, except Madura, they stand together first in the universe. The palace is full of interest, for it was here that the great events of the last three hundred years happened.'

Above, the Red Fort marked the apogee of Shah Jahan's building career and was his home for just nine years, until illness made him vulnerable to his sons' ambitions. He had lavished the most money on his private audience-hall, the riverside Diwan-i-Khas. Here, at either end of the central ceiling, he had the couplet of the fourteenth-century poet and saint, Amir Khusrau, inscribed in gilded letters: 'If on earth there be a paradise of bliss, It is this, Oh! It is this! It is this!'.

had made 'full use of all the resources of the sea and the mines'.

Most impressive of all, however, was the Diwan-i-Am (Public Audience Hall), where a vast awning 'of gold embroidered velvet' shaded the people who sat on the priceless carpets. 'This canopy was, according to the royal orders, woven in the imperial factory at Ahmedabad. . . it was erected on four silver poles, each of which was 22 yards high. It covered an area of 3,200 square yards, and 10,000 people could be accommodated under it.' Clearly it was the wonder of the event, for Samsam-ud-Daula continues: 'It took trained farashes and 3,000 additional men working hard for a month to erect it. In short, such a canopy – which resembled the heavens – had never been erected before, and such a building – which was a counterpart of the heavens – had never been decorated so elaborately.' Here the Emperor sat on a special throne, his princes and nobles on smaller ones, and distributed gifts and honours. Dara Shukoh, his eldest and favourite son, received a special khilat (robe of honour), an elephant, 200,000 rupees and an increased military rank.

Such splendour made the Court of Shah Jahan a marvel of the seventeenth-century world. With the Emperor's arrival, Court life blossomed and was quickly established. Within a year, a certain Chandar Bhan Brahman was writing: 'Its towers are the resting place of the sun . . . Its avenues are so full of pleasure that its lanes are like the road of paradise . . . Its climate is beautiful and pleasant.' From the start, the Red Fort's population was enormous, its administration a daily miracle. Niccolao Manucci reported that 'after any prince had left that emperor's court, taking with him as many as two hundred thousand men . . . it seemed as if not a single person had gone away.' Manucci did tend to exaggerate, but the impression is clear.

The Red Fort enjoyed its zenith under Shah Jahan and, for a few years, Aurangzeb. The daily life of this most luxurious of Courts amazed visitors, and through their diaries it comes to life. François Bernier (in India 1658–64), a French physician who wrote his account for the inquisitive Colbert, advised any reader who was 'a lover of good cheer . . . to quit Paris for the sake of visiting Delhi.' Other reports inspired Dryden to write his *Tragedy of Aurungzebe* (1675). Much later, Lovat Fraser compared Delhi favourably to London. 'Picture the roaring stream that converges upon the Mansion House, multiply it three times over . . . for the granite buildings familiar to every Londoner, you must imagine narrow counters, gorgeous with silks and brocades and heavy embroideries, so tempting and so costly . . . you must figure the broad avenue [of Chandni Chowk], with its umbrageous trees which the city of London can never hope to see . . . you must add the glaring lights, the masses of colour, the noise and the hubbub, the raucous conversations in stentorian tones which Cheapside knoweth not.'

The royal timetable was one of almost stultifying precision. Already, at Jahangir's itinerant Court, Sir Thomas Roe had remarked in Ajmer that the daily ritual was as 'regular as the clock that stricks at sett howers'. Now, under Shah Jahan's rule at the Red Fort, the clock kept equally good time. As the morning star appeared, the royal musicians played appropriate morning music and the muezzins of all the Delhi mosques – hardly a street or square was without one – called the faithful to prayer. By sunrise, a crowd of loyal citizens had gathered on the sands beneath the Jharokah–i Darshan (Showing Balcony) of the Khas Mahal where Jahangir slept. In a traditional ritual called Darshan, the Emperor presented himself to show he was alive and well; this was the moment when any citizen who felt he had been mistreated could put his complaint to the Emperor and seek redress. Meanwhile the royal horses, strong beasts from Turkey branded with the Emperor's mark, were being exercised outside the gates on the other side of the Fort, close to the tents pitched by the various rajas and chieftans in the Emperor's pay, who mounted guard in weekly turns; suspicious of their foreign ruler, they never slept inside the Fort walls.

The Emperor would then say his prayers and have breakfast. By mid-morning, the scene moved to the gilded and painted Diwan-i-Am where Bernier noted that 'the King gives audience indescriminately to all his subjects'. Here the Emperor sat up high on his throne on the marble plinth, the alcove behind him decorated with *pietra dura* birds, while eunuchs flapped away the flies with peacocks' tails. Papers and petitions were handed to him from the platform below; either side, his princes, ministers and courtiers assembled in strict rank for the day's public business, together with visiting ambassadors, all standing with eyes downcast, hands together. The public crowded into the courtyard to bring their requests and complaints before their ruler, or just to enjoy the spectacle and glimpse the royal glory.

The business took about two hours, contained a diverse selection of events, and

was staged and timed like a well-balanced royal gala performance. Reports from the Empire's outposts might be read aloud, or criminals might have their cases heard and, all too soon, their sentences proclaimed, for a row of executioners with hatchets and whips stood on hand to carry them out on the spot. The Emperor might inspect new royal horses and soldiers. And he would hear every petition brought by his people and, Bernier noted, 'often redress on the spot the wrongs of the aggrieved party'.

There were light interludes, too. The Emperor might listen to an account of a strange dream, or he might inspect elephants whose hides were scrubbed and then painted black and whose heads were painted with two red streaks right down the trunk. Each would be dressed in embroidered cloth and silver bells, with, as jewellery, valuable white cow-tails from Tibet hung from their ears. As each neared the throne, the mahout (driver) encouraged it to perform its party trick, bending one knee and lifting its trunk to roar aloud. Other animals kept for royal sport and show might follow: tame antelopes for fighting with each other, exotic rhinoceroses, buffaloes with huge horns for fighting lions and tigers, tame leopards and panthers used for hunting antelopes, and falcons and other birds of prey. The show might even include a review of some of the Emperor's more glamorous cavalry, decorated with fantastic trappings. Physical feats were shown off, too: a favourite was for a young man to slice through four bound sheep's feet using just a single swipe of a cutlass.

The arrival of an important visitor for his first audience with the Emperor was a highlight. As he came through the Naqqar Khana, his weapons were removed and he was announced by deafening drums, oboe-like instruments and cymbals – Bernier found it unbearable the first time, but it soon became a 'pleasure; in the night, when in bed and afar, on my terrace this music sounds in my ears as solemn, and melodious'. The visitor then approached the throne with deep salaams and presented the Emperor with nazarana, symbolic offerings of gold coins. In turn the Emperor's ministers dressed him in plush robes and, after the visitor had received presents in return for those he gave the Emperor, showed him to his allotted place. Throughout this most extraordinary programme there would be constant music and entertainment from jugglers, wrestlers, acrobats and dancing girls. Then, quite suddenly, the

Where brightly saried women now roam freely among the arches of the Diwan-i-Am, only Shah Jahan's highest-ranking courtiers could stand. When the traveller Jean de Thevenot attended, he remarked upon 'the great Hall . . . where the King (having all his Officers great and small standing before him, with their Hands a-cross their Breasts) gives every Day at noon Audience to all who have recourse to his Justice.'

Emperor pronounced 'takhlia', the red curtain dropped in front of his balcony and the show ended.

Despite the splendour, Bernier was horrified at 'the base and disgusting adulation which is invariably witnessed there. Whenever a word escapes the lips of the King . . . it is immediately caught by the surrounding throng; and the chief Omrahs (nobles of the Mughal court), extending their arms towards heaven, as if to receive some benediction, exclaim "Karamat! Karamat! wonderful! wonderful!"' And, he adds cynically: 'There is no Mogol who does not glory in repeating this proverb: Should the King say that it is night at noon, Be sure to cry, Behold, I see the moon!'

The rest of the Emperor's day was less public. He would retire from the Diwan-i-Am, leaving through the back into the quieter area of the Fort. There, in the Diwan-i-Khas (Private Audience Hall), he and his ministers would attend to the private business of the Empire. The air was cooled by breezes coming over the Yamuna, the walls were inlaid with precious stones, and the ceiling was coated with gilded flowers.

The legendary Peacock Throne was set up in the Diwan-i-Khas. On his accession, Shah Jahan had taken from his vast treasury a selection of precious stones and some gold and ordered the throne to be made, the chroniclers wrote, 'so beholders might benefit from their splendour . . . and Majesty might shine with increased brilliancy'. Seven years later it was ready: a large flat seat standing on legs, with four steps up to it and a canopy on top supported by twelve pillars, every surface encrusted with jewels. At the auspicious vernal equinox, Shah Jahan first sat on it; and when he moved to Delhi, the 'heavenly jewelled throne' was brought as part of the opening celebrations. Such self-indulgent extravagance had in it the seeds of decay. For a century, the throne was the glory of a decreasingly glorious empire, until in 1739 Nadir Shah carried it off to Persia as booty.

Jean-Baptiste Tavernier, a French jewel merchant who made five trips to India (between 1638 and 1668) buying gems and supplying them to Aurangzeb, naturally gave a detailed account of the Peacock Throne. It was, he said, the principal of the Emperor's seven thrones. Rubies, emeralds and diamonds were the chief stones, with plenty of gold and pearls around them. The rubies impressed him: 'there are about 108, all cabuchons, the least of which weighs 100 carats'. He thought the emeralds, at 30 to 60 carats each, were 'of good colour' but might have flaws, and

Left, the Emperor's ministers were not as bold as these young tourists, gazing up to the throne. François Bernier noted their behaviour: 'In the centre of the wall . . . and higher from the floor than a man can reach, is a wide and lofty opening, or large window, where the Monarch every day, about noon, sits upon his throne, with some of his sons at his right and left . . . Immediately under the throne is an enclosure, surrounded by silver rails, in which are assembled the whole body of Omrahs, the Rajas, and the Ambassadors, all standing, bent downward, and their hands crossed'. Because the throne was so high, ministers had to stand on the white marble dais which is inlaid with flora pietra dura designs in keeping with the rest of the throne.

Right, an Emperor's-eye view of his built-in throne in the Diwan-i-Am. From here it is possible to appreciate the richness and variety of the decoration. For example, the column of the baldachin is not just inlaid with floral and chevron designs; it is deeply carved as well. At the meeting of the column and canopy there is an explosion of baroque, exuberant carving. The canopy itself has six different borders combining carving and inlay, while the vault between it and the back wall has a completely different set of patterns. All this fine carving, these delicate clumps of blossoms and the fine, serpentine stems make a perfect foil to the bolder bird and flower panels set in the back wall.

Tourists flood in through the Naqqar Khana, just as Shah Jahan's subjects – and a good number of seventeenth-century tourists – did every day for the noontime audience in the Diwan-i-Am. The sandstone on this side of the drum house is richly carved with floral panels. The musicians which give it its name sat on the upper storey ready to strike up when any distinguished person arrived, at certain times of day, and merely at the Emperor's whim. The tourist-traveller François Bernier was greatly impressed by their instruments: 'To the ears of an European recently arrived, this music sounds very strangely, for there are ten or twelve hautboys, and as many cymbals, which play together. One of the hautboys, called a Karna, is a fathom and half in length . . . The cymbals of brass or iron are some of them at least a fathom in diameter. You may judge, therefore, of the roaring sound which issues from the Nagar-Kanay.' In fact, Bernier came to enjoy the music, although he noted that 'the Nagar'Kanay is . . . remote from the royal apartments, that the King may not be annoyed by the proximity of this music.'

he dismissed the diamonds as merely '10 to 12 carats in weight, all being showy stones, but very flat'. As to the peacock, surrounded with so much myth, Tavernier saw it clearly, above the canopy, 'with elevated tail made of blue sapphires . . . the body being of gold inlaid with precious stones, having a large ruby in front of the breast, from whence hangs a pear-shaped pearl of 50 carats or thereabouts'. What really impressed the French jeweller were the rows of huge round pearls, '6 to 10 carats each' set round each column.

To conclude the business of State, the most private discussions of all were reserved for a handful of trusted ministers and princes, and were held in the Emperor's Khas Mahal or Shah Burj (King's Tower). Then, exhausted, the Emperor retired to the Rang Mahal (Coloured Palace) or other rooms of his harem. Here, to the soothing tones of music or the soft sounds of a lady reading Urdu poetry, he would sit cross-legged on the silk carpets and dip his bejewelled fingers into some of the fifty or more dishes served up on gold, silver, jade or Chinese porcelain by the eunuchs, delivered by favourite ladies. Each dish arrived from the royal kitchens sealed, having been prepared by chefs so respected for their skills they were given the title maharaj (great king) and so jealous of their rivals they disclosed their recipes to none but their successors. Their delicacies might begin with a cooling sherbet flavoured with rose-petals to cleanse the tastebuds, followed by such delights as lambs' brains, quail, pheasant, river fish, sea tortoise, baby lamb and chicken, each tender morsel enriched with dried fruits, pounded nuts, ground spices and thick cream. To cool the tongue from the spices, there was creamy yoghurt, a constant flow of hot, freshly baked breads and mounds of golden rice given colour with expensive saffron and decorated with gossamer-thin sheets of silver, called varak. When the royal fingers were rinsed with perfumed water, there were sweet puddings and exotic fruits – favourites were mangoes in summer, melons in winter. To finish there was always aromatic spiced tea served in tiny, translucent, porcelain cups.

After a siesta, the Emperor would deal with the harem business. The harem was a huge and complex part of the palace, filling most of the southern half of the Fort and accounting for several hundred wives, sisters, widows and concubines, together with all their servants, eunuchs and general household. Furthermore, although Muslim women were not seen, the more powerful ones were often of considerable importance. Some ran estates or did extensive charity work, others ran trading or shipping businesses or dealt in gold and gemstones; and senior wives were politically influential and even held important seals of State. They all needed allowances, pensions and gifts for charitable dowries. The Emperor and his sons were the only men, apart from eunuchs, permitted in the harem, although physician travellers could slip in sometimes, if the Emperor was out of town. Bernier did just that, to visit a woman so ill she could not be moved, but 'a Kachemire shawl covered my head . . . and a eunuch led me by the hand'.

Manucci had a similar experience, but managed to give a better report. He found more bad than good qualities about the harem. Although 'they have permission' to dance and play, listen to romantic stories, 'recline on beds of flowers, to walk about in gardens, to listen to the murmur of the running waters, to hear singing, and other similar pastimes', doors were sealed and guarded at night and all visitors were recorded in writing. So jealous were Muslims, Manucci claimed, that 'some do not even trust their own brothers, and do not permit their women to appear before them . . . thus the women, being shut up and constantly watched, and having neither liberty nor occupation, think of nothing but adorning themselves, and their minds dwell on nothing but malice and lewdness'. And as typical Manucci gossip, he adds that some even 'affect the invalid, simply that they may have the chance of some conversation with, and have their pulse felt by, the physician. The latter stretches out his hand inside the curtain; they lay hold of it, kiss it, and softly bite it. Some, out of curiosity, apply it to their breast, which has happened to me several times.'

The harem business done, the Emperor performed Darshan (showing to the people) once more. Then it was time for amusements such as watching an elephant fight, the exclusive privilege of the Emperor. Staged on the sands between the Fort and the Yamuna, the palace terraces provided grandstand seats for him and his favourite courtiers – and courtesans, who could peek out from the Rang Mahal. The traveller Peter Mundy (in India 1628–33) described such spectacles, when the beasts would be 'of the fairest bignesse and strongest, whose teeth are sawan off in the midle and then bound about with iron or Brass'. Each had a 'guide sitting on his Neck. Att the word given they are lett goe, and soe running one against the other with their Truncks aloft they meete head to head. There they with their teeth lye

The wall of the east side of the Naqqar Khana, facing the Diwan-i-Am, is entirely carved with floral panels. These three panels are especially fine. Although the flowers appear to be identifiable, botanists conclude that the realism is misleading and most Mughal artists abstracted their flower designs from basic types, such as a lily, poppy or rose.

Above, the mirrored and plastered ceilings of the Emperor's most private palace, the Khas Mahal, would have reflected the brightly coloured silks worn by him and his trusted ministers as they discussed the most intimate matters of state. Around the mirror pieces and beneath them, it is possible to identify the great floral designs and bold arabesques which would have been painted and gilded.

Below, inside the Bhadaun pavilion of the Hayat Bakhsh garden, all is marble. Here the royal courtiers would come and sit to catch the breezes and enjoy the perfumes of the surrounding jasmine and other specially selected, strong-scented blossoms. The richly carved back wall — its pietra dura stones sadly ravaged — sets the scene for the central pool. In this, little oil lamps would be lit in the niches and their flickering flames would reflect in the water at the bottom, which already glowed with the coloured stones of the pietra dura floral inlay.

Opposite, leaving through the back door of the throne in the Diwan-i-Am, the Emperor had direct access to the quieter, less public area of the Fort. Outside the door, he could look across the courtyards, where there is now an open garden, to his Khas Mahal on the right and his Diwan-i-Khas on the left, usually his next stop to conduct intimate state business.

Thrustinge and forceinge with all their strength', until their keepers part them with 'fireworks on long Bamboes, whose cracks and noyse, fire and smoake doe sever them, soe lett them joyne againe' until one wins, 'thrusting him with his teeth, tramplinge and overlyeing him, for they can neither kick, bite nor Scratch'.

The Emperor's day ended with prayers, a family dinner and, perhaps, a return visit to the harem to listen to music, play with his children, watch dancing and generally enjoy himself. For the rest of the Emperor's family, retinue and the hundreds of courtiers living in the Red Fort, amusements were concentrated in the gardens with their fountains and in the many bazaars. And wherever they roamed, the canals of the Nahr-i Bihisht that fed the gardens and cooled the palaces were twinkling with an extra royal extravagance, for the heads of the fish that swam in them were fitted with gold rings set with rubies and seed-pearls.

Sometimes there was a special festival, an excuse for even more pomp and ceremony than on a usual day. At Diwali (the Festival of Lights), the Fort and the whole city sparkled with fireworks, and the parapets, walls and window-ledges of every building glowed with tiny oil lamps. The Marchioness of Dufferin and Ava was thrilled when she saw the spectacle in 1885: 'Can you imagine a whole city traced out in lines of light? It was beautiful.'

But the most special celebrations were reserved for the Emperor's birthday. Jean de Thévenot (1633–86), who travelled the Orient extensively, was in Delhi for one of Aurangzeb's: 'During five days there is great rejoycing all over the town . . . which is exprest by presents, feastings, bonefires and dances'. The Emperor would be weighed on huge scales against gold, silver and jewels which were then distributed to his people; Bernier notes how 'all the courtiers expressed much joy when it was found that Aureng-Zebe weighed two pounds more than the year preceding'; Thévenot was more sceptical and reckoned the bales of treasure 'were so closely packed that one cannot see what is within them . . . then they weigh the King with a great many things that are good to eat; and I believe that what is within the bales is not a whit more precious'. Both men remarked on the fabulous decorations: the two audience halls were done up in 'a canopy of brocade with deep fringes of gold', all the royal apartments hung with floral satin canopies and 'large tassels of silk and gold', the floors coated with silk carpets 'of immense length and breadth', the 'fairest elephants decked with the richest trappings', and a special huge tent pitched for extra guests and lined with floral chintzes 'so natural and colours so vivid, that the tent seemed to be encompassed with real parterres'. Omrahs competed to decorate the most beautiful gallery and to give the Emperor the most ostentatious present; the most beautiful women of the harem staged a fair, princesses dressing up as traders to flirt with their Emperor.

Ordinary daily life outside the Fort walls was pretty hectic and the city vibrated with action day and night. About five miles outside the walls were the sarais, inns for merchants, scholars, religious men and other travellers. Each, like a mini town, was equipped with barbers, tailors, blacksmiths, dancing girls, and rooms for about a thousand visitors. Others crammed inside a city that was full to bursting when the Court was in town, slightly more spacious when it left. Indeed, life in the city reflected that in the Red Fort.

The most impressive visitor to the Court was an ambassador, for his arrival through the streets and then his performance at the public Diwan-i-Am combined the most exotic robes and the most extravagant diplomatic present-giving, for each knew that 'those who bring the largest present and the heaviest purse are the most acceptable, the best received and the soonest attended to'. Furthermore, their clever, flattering choice of presents revealed much about the taste, querks, passions and lifestyle of the Emperors. The Uzbeks and Persians, both high-ranking diplomats, are good examples. When the Uzbek ambassadors came before Aurangzeb, each was honoured with a serapah, a top-to-toe outfit of brocade vest, turban and silk sash. In turn, they presented just what the Emperor wanted: boxes of expensive lapis lazuli stones – much-prized for use in *pietra dura* inlay and for grinding down to the finest blue pigment for miniature paintings; some long-haired camels and Turkish horses for processions, travelling and battle; camel-loads of dried fruits including prunes, apricots and three types of raison, essential ingredients of the rich Mughlai cuisine; and quantities of apples, pears, grapes and melons – all favourite Delhi winter treats.

The Persians did even better. For them, the city bazaars through which they processed were redecorated, Aurangzeb's cavalry stood either side, and musicians and Omrahs accompanied them along their way. At the Diwan-i-Am, they presented

25 extremely fine horses and 20 equally good camels; many cases of rosewater to perfume the royal fountains and the cooling royal sherbets; some beidmichk, a rare cordial and another Mughal favourite; half a dozen carpets 'of great size and beauty' for relaxing comfortably and sumptuously in the Red Fort palaces; and some fine brocade, Damascus cutlasses and sets of horse furnishings 'of superior richness, ornamented with superb embroidery and with small pearls, and very beautiful turqoises'.

The Europeans, who badly wanted to trade with India, came too. Sir Thomas Roe had arrived at Jahangir's court in 1616 with quite the wrong presents; only the paintings and, finally, a glass coach and English gloves seem to make any impression. But Adrian, the Dutch ambassador, who had run a factory at Surat on the west coast, measured up Mughal taste precisely when he came to do business with Aurangzeb in Delhi. First, to gain access to the Emperor, he greased the ministers' palms with gold, silver and fine cloth, then he presented the Emperor with one vast length of scarlet cloth and another of green, large mirrors, quantities of earthenware dishes, Japanese paintings, a little throne and Chinese and Japanese china. The Mughals especially prized the pale green celadon ware for its resemblance to expensive jade. But it was the dainty, painted throne which amused Aurangzeb most, so much so that he had it covered with glass to protect it from dust.

Just as the citizens took part in the ritual and economic life of the Fort, so the Emperor and his family took an active part in the city life. For pleasure and refuge against summer heat and dust, several of the city's lush gardens were laid out and maintained by royals. Of the three principal bazaars – all royal procession routes – the greatest was Chandni Chowk (Moonlit Square). It was a favourite for royal, religious and wedding processions: a minor noble marriage procession might easily be a mile long and include elephants, horses, camels, drummers, trumpeters, dancing girls and hundreds of family, friends and hangers-on, all dressed sumptuously in the brightest coloured silks, the groom wearing a golden turban with a great plume.

The first section of Chandni Chowk served members of the imperial household, servants, clerks and artisans. The next part was the financial section, known as Ashrafi Bazar (Moneychangers' Bazaar), and included the square whose moon-

The most private of the Emperor's political discussions could take place in the royal Hammams, prestigious rooms which merited a riverside site next to the Diwan-i-Khas and were lavishly decorated. Babur had noted in his diary that three things annoyed him about Hindustan, 'one was its heat, another its strong winds, the third is the dust. Baths were the means of removing all three inconveniences.'

Here, the central marble bath, fed by the Nahr-i Bihisht, is fitted with a seat for the Emperor and his ministers. Surrounding it, instead of a silk carpet, there is a marble one of pietra dura. More refreshing water flows along a narrow channel around the edge, while delicate pietra dura flowers decorate the dado — and still retain their stones.

A closer look at one corner of this thoroughly royal marble bathroom reveals the sophisticated designs of several pietra dura *patterns, which are then placed side by side with perfect taste and colour sense. The main floor covering is a feathery fretwork enclosing flowerheads of grey, red and mustard yellow, contrasting with the cartouches of the border. Next to this is the water canal with bold herringbone stripes of black, grey and honey-brown, quite different from the pencil-fine curling flower stems at the bottom of the wall.*

reflecting pool gave the whole street its name. Here Jahanara built a Hammam (baths) on the south side, in the jewellery quarter, and on the north side she laid out a garden and built an in-town sarai with 'beautifully painted and appointed' rooms. Her guests, she insisted, were only the richest of the top merchants, the Persians and Uzbeks. At the far end of the street, Fatepuri Masjid was added by Nawab Fathpuri Begum, one of Shah Jahan's senior wives.

Early in the eighteenth century, Dargah Kuli Khan marvelled at the rubies, emeralds and pearls on sale, the elegant glass huqqas (hookahs, smoking pipes) and eyeglasses and the rich sweetmeats; other travellers noticed the kebabs, the scented flowers, the ever-present astrologers and the coffee houses, a Persian import where amirs (high-ranking Court officials) met to chat, debate and listen to poetry. Bernier marvelled at the fruits on sale – dry fruits from Samarkand, mangoes ('the best come from Bengale, Golkonda and Goa'), and 'admirable melons . . . nothing is considered so great a treat: it forms the chief expense of the Omrahs'. Even this century, Rupert Croft-Cooke wrote in 1969 that he thought Chandni Chowk 'a microcosm of India' and would never tire of walking 'from the Red Fort to the cool fruit market at the far end'.

Under Shah Jahan and Aurangzeb, the citizens could be sure of at least one royal procession a week, when the Emperor made his way along Khas Bazar (Special Bazaar) to the Jama Masjid. Every Friday, when he processed there to pray, the route was spruced up for his majesty. François Bernier was impressed by the whole event: 'the streets through which he passes are watered to lay the dust and temper the heat'. Soldiers lined the way, horsemen ensured it was kept clear of people, until at the right moment 'his Majesty leaves the fortress, sometimes on an elephant, decorated with rich trappings, and a canopy supported by painted and gilt pillars; and sometimes in a throne gleaming with azure and gold, placed on a litter covered with scarlet or brocade, which eight chosen men carry on their shoulders'. Omrahs followed, and hoards of bejewelled nobles and courtiers made sure they were seen to be worshipping, too. And crowds cheered on another hour of lavish spectacle in the capital of the great Mughal Empire.

Above, from the top of Aurangzeb's barbican in front of Lahore Gate, Chandni Chowk stretches out westwards, the great view closed at the far end by Fatehpuri Masjid. Bicycle rickshaws, auto-rickshaws, tongas, bicycles, scooters and cars jostle with hundreds of pedestrians with hoots, honks, cheers and cries to fight their way up and down. This is still Shahjahanabad's – or Old Delhi's – principal thoroughfare, although the north-south highway in the foreground has sliced it off from its parent Fort. All religions are represented here: the pink and white Digamber Jain Temple and Charity Bird Hospital are in the first building on the left; the Sikhs' Sisganj Gudwara, the Muslims' Sonehri Masjid and many others follow. And the street is steeped in history. Here Nadir Shah stood on 11 March, 1739 to watch his men massacre most of Delhi's inhabitants and ravage the city in just six hours. Here Aurangzeb exhibited his captive older brother, Dara Shukoh alive on an elephant and later, in 1659, exhibited his corpse, to warn any supporters to rethink their loyalties. Here the British hanged freedom fighters and exhibited the corpses of three princes in 1857 for the same reasons.

Right, down at the west end of Chandni Chowk, the Kashmiri dried fruit and nut merchants still keep their tiny kiosk shops in the walls of Fatehpuri Masjid. This merchant sits among his carefully displayed dishes of fresh and succulent cashewnuts, pistachios, walnuts and almonds.

On Fridays, the Emperor paraded through the streets and along Khas Bazar to enter the eastern, royal entrance of the Jama Masjid for prayers.

Architectural Wonder of the World

3

'After Jahangir came Shah Jahan. In his reign came the climax of Moghal splendour, and in his reign also are clearly visible the seeds of decay . . . And yet much, perhaps, may be forgiven him for the marvels of loveliness in stone and marble that he has left behind. It was in his time that Moghal architecture reached its height. Besides the Taj, he built the Moti Masjid – the Pearl Mosque in Agra; and the great Jami Masjid of Delhi, and the Diwan-i-am and Diwan-i-khas in the palace in Delhi. These are buildings of noble simplicity; some of them enormous and yet graceful and elegant, and fairy-like in their beauty.' Jawaharlal Nehru, *Glimpses of World History*, 1934–5

The Red Fort is extraordinary for being a palace-fortress laid out from scratch following a single, ordered plan; for the survival of its most important buildings and its city setting; and for the quality of those buildings. Moreover, according to contemporary records, its instigator, Shah Jahan, both designed and personally directed the more important parts. As Nehru observed, the buildings mingle simplicity, elegance and fairy-tale beauty. Despite the ravages of three and a half centuries, enough has survived to bear testament to what was, until the turmoil of 1857, a wonder of the world.

The basic layout of the Fort is simple. Just as Shahjahanabad divided into ordinary (city) and special (Red Fort) areas, so the Fort itself was similarly divided. The pivotal building is the Diwan-i-Am (Public Audience Hall). West of it lies the ordinary area, with the greatest public access: here are the bazaars, the offices, other Fort services and the two gateways into the city, Lahore and Delhi. Special permission was needed to get beyond the west side of the Diwan-i-Am. North of it lie the semi-private palace gardens, with important courtiers' mansions beyond – although top princes and wives had their own palaces outside the Fort walls. East of it is the private palace area, the range of marble apartments along the east side of the Fort. South of it is the most private area of all, the harem. Throughout, every detail is formal and regular, using an extensive grid network of squares: there is hardly a curve or diagonal line.

Within this plan, each building is placed according to its function. The Fort was both home and office for the Emperor, and its domestic and official functions

The controversial panel of Orpheus charming the beasts is in the back wall of the Diwan-i-Am. This western iconography, copied from a painting by Raphael, has its origins in the Roman catacombs. But whereas the catacomb artist gave the god a lyre, Raphael gave him a violin, as has this craftsman – probably an Italian. And the pietra dura technique of the rest of the wall also seems to have some direct Italian influence. Although the basic technique was brought from Persia by the Mughals, it is possible that Italian craftsmen introduced their refined pictorial skills to India when they worked for Shah Jahan at Agra. It is still debated whether Italian or Agra craftsmen created this.

Above, a camera lens improves on the human eye to show the full glory of the view down Chatta Chowk. Lahore Gate is at the front. In Shah Jahan's time, before Aurangzeb added his barbican, citizens of Shahjahanabad could have seen the crisply chiselled sandstone and the enticing bustle of the bazaar within. Today, one curious visitor feels the great gates which were slammed shut at night. Beyond, the bazaar still bubbles with life, but with fewer jewellery shops and more light-hearted Indian handicrafts shops. Half-way down, a break in the roof provides the bazaar with soft light. A pool of harsh sunlight indicates the area of the Jilau Khana, and the sun-beaten sandstone wall is the Naqqar Khana. Beyond that, it is just possible to see the great white marble throne in the distant Diwan-i-Am.

Below, the plain, west side of the Naqqar Khana was as far as some visitors got. Entry to the Diwan-i-Am courtyard was strictly controlled — and these tourists appear to be waiting, too. But it is possible to glimpse the Diwan-i-Am through the arch and across what used to be the courtyard. And the strong-sighted can see the Emperor's white marble throne in the shadows inside the cusped arch.

Above, the first view of the Diwan-i-Am after passing through the Naqqar Khana, remains unobstructed, but the buildings enclosing the Diwan-i-Am courtyard have long since gone. When Shah Jahan held his morning court here, his subjects crammed into this great courtyard and peered over each others' heads to catch a glimpse of the Emperor. The central scalloped arch of the arcade is slightly wider to emphasize its importance, and through it the great royal throne is just visible in the shadows.

Below, one of several wall-paintings of trees, some bearing fruit, which decorate the deep tunnel of the Naqqar Khana.

reflected what the historian Stephen P. Blake calls 'the patrimonial-bureaucratic' nature of Mughal rule. The intimate relationship of the delicate private palace buildings to each other is in strong contrast to the great public vista that leads from Lahore gate through Naqqar Khana to the bold Diwan-i-Am. Agra and Lahore could boast glorious, refined private palaces, but neither city could offer such impressive public areas, such stage-sets for the ostentatious theatre of kingship, and neither city could continue the palace plan into the wide streets found at Delhi. The Red Fort is therefore above all a theatrical symbol of power and wealth, albeit a most sophisticated and beautiful one.

It begins with the fearsome walls. They trace an elongated octagonal shape almost two miles long and 60 to 75 feet high, with a base width of 45 feet tapering to 30 feet at the top. Battlements and, originally, 21 towers add to their strength; these and the four gateways and two entrances break the visual monotony. A wide moat, 75 feet wide and 30 feet deep, further protects the Fort on all but the river side; and visually, it emphasizes its separate status from the city. The 124 acres inside are, as contemporary recorders eagerly pointed out, twice that of Akbar's Agra Fort.

Four gateways led through the walls into the Fort, symbolizing the change from ordinary to special areas of the city, and each had a different function. The eastern one, on the riverside beneath the Jharokah-i Darshan, was the principal entrance to the Diwan-i-Khas; it was through this that Shah Jahan first entered his completed city in 1648. The northern one led across Jahangir's bridge to Salimgarh Fort. The southern and western were, and are, the two main entrances from the city. The first was called Akbarabadi (now Delhi) Gate and led to the Jama Masjid and, through Faiz Bazar, out of the city onto the road to Agra. The second was Lahore Gate, leading through Chandni Chowk and onto the road to Lahore. Giant elephants carved of Chittor stone and brought from Agra stood in front of Delhi Gate, keeping guard, and considered idolatrous by Aurangzeb, who removed them (although they were renewed by Lord Curzon in 1903). Aurangzeb also built the barbicans in front of both gates, strengthening their defences but blocking out the visual relationship between city and Fort.

Lahore Gate already has the Shah Jahan stamp of royal refinement: the barely decorated sandstone soars up for three storeys between two semi-octagonal towers, topped by a delicate, seven-arch arcade with white domes, flanked by two minarets. It was the principal and the ceremonial entrance (and is now the only public one); Aurangzeb later made it the headquarters of his Qiladar (Fort Commander). In front was a large space, the part hard by the moat planted with a lush garden of roses and grapes, and the rest occupied by an overspill of the life inside: here Rajput chiefs camped while doing their stint of guard duty, horses entering the Emperor's service were inspected and grooms exercised the royal horses.

A pointed arch leads into the shadows of Chatta Chowk, or Bazar-i Mussaqaf (Covered Bazaar) or Meena Bazar (Gold Bazar), considered by architectural historian James Fergusson, writing in 1910, 'the noblest entrance known to belong to any existing palace'. The Fort's nobles and courtesans came here and, shaded from the sun, wandered the 270-feet long arcade lined with two storeys of shops and the odd Persian coffee house, and fed with light and air half way along, where there is an octagonal square. The whole structure, although of a design common to West Asia, was an innovation in India. Shah Jahan had heard about the arcade in Isfahan, and it seems that when he saw one at Peshawar (between Lahore and Kabul) he was so impressed he ordered the Red Fort's to be modelled on it. Muhammad Salih loyally gives him full credit for designing it 'with effortless attention and unique building talent'. Whether or not its design was original, Chatta Chowk is certainly a brilliant piece of architecture and an essential part of a visitor's progress towards the royal presence, on a direct line to the Diwan-i-Am. This is the great vista of the Red Fort: through the dark tunnel the Naqqar Khana (Drum House) is just visible, and through that lies the Diwan-i-Am; turning back pre-Aurangzeb visitors looked down the central city thoroughfare, Chandni Chowk.

The majority of the Fort's administrative population lived between Lahore Gate and the Naqqar Khana. One can imagine how Chatta Chowk opened into a large enclosed square, the Jilau Khana (Forecourt), with a rectangular pool in the centre. The sides were lined with tiny rooms housing the amirs of the daily guard, except in the south-west corner, where the wazir (superintendent) of the imperial household had his offices. Long, unvaulted bazaars led off to left (to nobles' residences) and right (to Delhi Gate), lined with two storeys of retail shops and workshops, where craftsmen serving the royal household practised embroidery, painting, tailoring and,

The back wall of the Emperor's built-in throne in the Diwan-i-Am is a masterpiece of design and technique and is perhaps the finest piece of Mughal *pietra dura* work on a grand scale. The entire white marble wall shimmers with a single, intricate design. Either side of the Emperor's doors are two vast marble sheets. The one above is inlaid with three central bird panels surrounded by a coil of delicate floral arabesques; the one below has two central vases of flowers. The lunette above the doors has the Indian hoopoe and other birds flying and perched among fruiting boughs which surround two rows of larger bird panels, topped with one showing Orpheus charming the beasts. In the border running around the whole wall, the birds and flowers are joined by delightful lions.

Four panels from the back wall of the throne in the Diwan-i-Am. Although birds and flowers look very realistic in Mughal art, ornothologists and botanists have concluded that they are usually abstract, slightly fanciful designs based on real life rather than identifiable types. These panels are of dark grey limestone, probably found locally, while the mustard-yellow band is kurkura, a limestone quarried near Jaisalmer. The flower stem is abur stone, a hard

limestone also quarried near Jaisalmer, up by the Pakistan border; and turquoise-topped stamens poke out of the cornelian petals. A pair of butterflies dance around one bird, the top one with lapis and cornelian wings, the bottom one with beautifully patterned onyx marble wings. The fruit of this branch is possibly the same onyx, while the bird has high-grade lapis in his striped tail-feathers and a much coarser, mottled lapis for his breast.

of course, goldsmithing. In the centre of the far side stood the Naqqar Khana (Drum House), in the square where bureaucrats, petitioners, ministers and others gathered in the hope of attending the daily audience in the Diwan-i-Am, tantilizingly near on the other side of the Naqqar Khana. And this was as far as some of them got.

The Naqqar Khana, also known as Naubat-Khana, regulated entry to the centre stage of the Red Fort. It both controlled who was or was not admitted, and how they were admitted – only grand arrivals were serenaded by musicians playing on the upper floors, and only princes could ride through on horseback. (The gate was also called Hathipol, as those riding elephants [hathi] were obliged to dismount, too.) And as it was the only entrance, it dictated the manner in which each person first saw that splended stage – head on. On the Jilau Khana side of Naqqar Khana, three bold arches break up the almost flat wall, the central one the entrance; to contrast, nine delicately cusped arches are strung along the upper storey. The rectangular building is then deep enough for the entrance to create, as at the Taj Mahal, a strong sense of progressing from one mood through darkness into another, in this case from a public to a rarified one. The transition is emphasized by the delicate wall-paintings of fruiting trees, which are still visible inside the gateway. More extravagant decoration coats the wall facing Diwan-i-Am, every inch of red sandstone sculpted with fine relief of cartouches, arabesques and blossoming lilies, roses, poppies and other flowers, each of which was originally gilded. In all, the Naqqar Khana employs all the theatrical, practical and visual devices of the entrance to a walled Mughal garden tomb, such as Humayun's or the Taj Mahal.

Supremely elegant, the Diwan-i-Am stands opposite. It was originally sited on the far side of an enclosed courtyard – again, one must imagine both the courtyard and the sumptuously decorated apartments lining it, where the amirs of the standing guard were quartered. The Diwan-i-Am was the Mughal Empire's centre stage for displaying its greatest pomp and ceremony. Here, in front of his people, the Emperor dealt with the routine military, administrative and financial matters of state. The building is really an open pavilion. On a low platform measuring 185 by 70 feet, forty pillars three bays deep support nine-cusped arches beneath a wide chajja (eave) and plain parapet. The double columns along the front and down both sides help define the space. Seen from the Naqqar Khana the façade is strikingly effective: a row of

A few stones survive to give an idea of how this centrepiece of the Rang Mahal would have looked in Shah Jahan's time, water shooting up into the air from the fountain and tinkling down into the lotus-shaped pool with its three colourful borders. Behind it, the lattice-work of the triple window, the trompe-l'œil carved roofs above them and the vestiges of painted gold arabesques above all hint at the magnificence of the original decoration. Lovat Fraser wrote in 1902 that 'only by degrees do you realise how much of the first fine splendour has vanished . . . the jewelled walls of the Zenana glittered in the morning light . . . Underground passages permitted the royal favourites to wander from the Zenana to the baths unseen by curious eyes . . . The very baths were richly inlaid and jewelled. In one, dozens of little fountains spurted rosewater, wherein the royal ladies dipped their jewels on rising.'

nine perfectly modulated arches, the central one slightly larger, rests on columns whose capitals are carved with voluptuous leaves; the deeply overhanging chajja creates a dark shadow in the bright sunlight and emphasizes the strong horizontality, given further weight by the plain parapet above. At the same time, the building's slim platform and the corner roof chhatris (pavilions), originally gilded, prevent it from being ponderous.

The Diwan-i-Am at Fatehpur Sikri is still an enclosed courtyard, but the essential public stage is by comparison thoroughly modest and the Emperor would have been quite difficult to see behind the jali screens. Agra's more open stage was a closer model for Delhi, and it was the daily crush of citizens through Agra's north gate which, among other reasons, inspired Shah Jahan to build a fresh palace of the scale and size suited to his Court. But the clean, restrained lines of the Diwan-i-Am must be seen in context. All surfaces were originally stuccoed or painted and gilded, and it seems that the sandstone walls were coated with chunam, a fine polished plaster whose ingredient of ground eggshell helps give it an almost marble quality. The dazzling white pavilion and courtyard were then strewn with carpets, while hangings were suspended from the (surviving) iron rings fitted beneath the chajja. And three railings separated the throng into strict hierarchy: a stone one in front of the pavilion for minor officials, a five-foot-high silver one inside the pavilion for major officials, and a gold one inside this for the princes, high-ranking ministers and ambassadors.

The Emperor's high marble baldachin survives, as does the marble platform beneath it, where nobles handed petitions, complaints and papers to him. Both have areas of *pietra dura* inlay, but it is the niche behind the throne that gives a hint of the original total effect. It is a remarkable panel of complex *pietra dura* work, showing birds perched on floral boughs topped by a panel after a Raphael painting of Orpheus playing a violin and charming the beasts. The panel was surely made by an Italian craftsman and either worked on site or acquired as a masterpiece by Shah Jahan. The Diwan-i-Am was the furthest the public and minor officials penetrated into the Red Fort. Behind the pavilion and across gardens lay the more private palace buildings, accessible via a corridor running from the centre of the left side of the courtyard. To the right lay the very private harem.

The harem covered almost a third of the area of the Red Fort. It stretched from

The Nahr-i Bihisht is the continuous element in the string of marble palaces, only its floors varying in patterning from building to building. Here it flows over plain marble slabs from the Khas Mahal down towards the Rang Mahal. This side of the Khas Mahal has an open portico facing the ladies' palace. Inside the central arch, beyond the marble bridge, the canal widens into a pool to give additional soothing coolness to the air, and the magnificent carved screen closing the sleeping rooms is just visible behind. Every inch of the portico walls is densely patterned with carved marble and vestiges of full-blown, blue chrysanthemums, while two very delicate pieces of jali work form the windows above the doors to inner rooms.

From the east side, the Diwan-i-Khas appears to sit lightly on the wall, belying both its massive weight of marble and its historical importance. The beautifully balanced façade is divided into five openings, with a blind arcade carved above two pairs of windows and a central triple one. It was behind this window that Shah Jahan sat in glory on his Peacock Throne. But the Diwan-i-Khas was later to witness some of the Mughal empire's most tragic events. In 1739 Nadir Shah plundered Muhammad Shah's Delhi and carried off the Peacock Throne to Persia. In 1788 the Rohilla Chief, Ghulam Qadir

Khan, blinded Shah Alam II and dug up the palace floors in search of buried treasure. And here in 1858 the British tried the last Emperor, Bahadur Shah II, 'ignominiously for murder', as Wilfred Blunt, a great nationalist, learnt from an old dentist. 'He saw this last of the Mogul kings crouched before the Military Commission, dressed in a piece of sacking and a coarse turban, ''like a coolie''. Here, too, the English soldiers slew and destroyed some thousands of innocent men in revenge for the death of about one hundred. Such are the resources of civilization.'

Azad Burj (Lion Tower) up to the Rang Mahal, its principal apartment, which stands on the riverside directly behind the Diwan-i-Am. It is difficult to know exactly what the harem looked like, as few people could enter its doors. Its life was veiled in secrecy and, tragically, the British destroyed most of it after they retook Delhi in 1858. However, the architectural historian James Fergusson, writing in 1910, acquired a reliable 'native plan' which revealed that 'it contained three garden courts, and some thirteen or fourteen other courts, arranged some for state, some for convenience'. He adds that, considering the beauty of the Agra ladies' apartments, these 'must have vied with the public apartments in richness and in beauty'. Bernier relied on hearsay for his description of large and small 'beautiful apartments . . . according to the rank and income of the females. Nearly every chamber has its reservoir of running water at the door ; on every side are gardens, delightful alleys, shady retreats, streams, fountains, grottoes . . . lofty divans and terraces on which to sleep coolly at night'. Other sources tell of coloured paving stones and fountains in tree-filled gardens fed by the Nahr-i Bihisht.

The two surviving buildings are Jahanara Begum's mansion (also known as Mumtaz Mahal and now the Archaeological Museum) and Rang Mahal, both on the riverside. The building between them, Daria Mahal, has gone, as has the one south of them on the riverside, Khurd Jahan. The Begum's marble mansion has jali screen windows to ensure privacy. Inside, the cusped arches of its six apartments still have vestiges of bold, almost heraldic, floral designs, and the walls have traces of inlaid glasswork. Near it was the Khwaspurah (Special Quarter), reserved for female members of the harem who did not have royal lineage.

The Rang Mahal (Coloured Palace) or Imtiaz Mahal (Palace of Pre-eminence) is, like the Diwan-i-Am, a pivotal building, this time between the harem and the Emperor's private apartments. It needs to be seen first from the garden in the context of its neighbours, the Khas Mahal, the Diwan-i-Khas and the Hammams. This the apogee of Mughal building: a string of finely proportioned palace buildings constructed of extravagant white marble, raised up on platforms, their perfect shapes silhouetted against the harsh blue Indian sky. These are the 'marvels of loveliness' Nehru wrote of. The Diwan-i-Am had restrained stateliness; these buildings exude lyrical luxuriance. Each is different and yet each is in harmony with the

The Mughal visitor's first view of the all-marble, extravagant
Diwan-i-Khas would have been similar to this, except he would have
entered through the only doorway into the innermost of the Fort's
maze of courtyards — and furnishings of brightly coloured hangings
and rugs would have contrasted with the dazzling white. The
scalloped arcade and the rooftop chhatris relieve the crisp but slightly
ponderous horizontals of the chajja and parapet. And through the
central arch it is possible to see the low dais where the Emperor sat
enthroned.

The floral panels of the Diwan-i-Khas piers were probably made by Agra craftsmen, many of whom had worked on the Taj Mahal and the Fort at Agra before coming up to Delhi. The flower designs are a little more spare than at Agra, and the Chinese clouds either side of the big blossom are an innovation. Both design and materials were supplied by a merchant to the workshop chief, a master craftsman. The marble slabs were passed from craftsman to craftsman in the workshop, each contributing his speciality — marble-cutting, gem-setting or chiselling — until the piece was complete and ready for polishing. In this painstakingly slow work, one slip meant the piece was ruined.

others. The group is quite unlike the palaces at Agra and Lahore, which had to make the best of a site occupied by earlier buildings. Here, the virgin site provided an opportunity for building on a single level and for considered spacing, giving the Delhi group a new order. One must imagine their connecting courts, corridors and formal gardens, and lavish decoration, but the principal connecting and decorative element survives: the Nahr-i Bihisht (Stream of Paradise) which flowed down the centre of them all, its channel decorated differently in each palace but most finely in the Rang Mahal. Its waters cooled the air, soothed the eye and gave added twinkle and luxuriance to the gilded and mirrored decoration.

Built for the senior queens, the Rang Mahal is the largest building of the group and was the centre of social activity. Like the Diwan-i-Am, it is basically a pavilion and measures 153 by 69 feet. The façade has five great nine-cusped arches (originally fitted with jali screens for privacy) between two almost plain ends, all shaded by a deep chajja and topped by delicate corner chhatris. The central arch is slightly wider, and through it the Nahr-i Bihisht poured down over the two rows of niches, lit with candles, into a formal garden. Either side of these niches the platform has jali screens letting air into its cool basement rooms.

Inside, there are six apartments. The central area has eight square piers arranged in two rows supporting more cusped arches. Four central piers surround a large, lotus-shaped, marble pool with three deep borders of *pietra dura* floral inlay, all once brought to life under the bubbling waters of the central fountain. The riverside wall has square windows at floor height flanking a central triple window surrounded by gold cartouches – the low windows enabled the ladies, reclining on carpets against bolsters, to get the full benefit of any breezes. The dado is marble, as are the blind niches on the pillars; other surfaces, now white, were brightly painted and gilded – vestiges survive on the central arch at the front. The effect of the great sweeps of the arches from every viewpoint combined with what Percy Brown called the 'sinuous scrolls and serpentine lines' of the painted decoration to help create an atmosphere of utter luxury. Indeed, a contemporary chronicler claimed that 'in lustre and in colour it is far superior to the palaces in the promised paradise'.

A pair of small, cube-sized rooms lurk either side of this hall, found through arches plastered with bold cartouche patterns. These rooms were known as Khas Khanas

(Reed Houses), because they were lined with blinds of sweet-smelling wet reeds to cool the air and fight the punishing heat. But they also gained the nickname Shish Mahal (Mirror Palace) for their mirrorwork ceilings, which reflected both the gurgling waters of the canal and the flickering candlelight – ideas found at Agra and in the Rajput forts of Rajasthan. Their walls have panels of floral plasterwork. The canal flows between these rooms, ending at the southern wall where a triple-arched marble window closes the vista through all three marble palaces.

The Khas Mahal (Special Palace) is next door, small and anonymous by comparison to the great Rang Mahal. Here were the Emperor's most personal rooms, known as his Aramgah (Place of Rest). The simple exterior belies the rich interior. This gem epitomizes privacy and intimacy. The façade overlooking the garden merely has square panels in relief and some jali screens, with no fancy rooftop chhatris; a closed courtyard lay this way. North and south façades are more open, with arcades facing towards the Diwan-i-Khas for business and the Rang Mahal for pleasure. And the east façade protrudes out from the Fort to catch all available draughts.

The cooling waters of the Nahr-i Bihisht dominated the interior. In the central three rooms, known as the Khwabgah (Sleeping Chamber), the canal's twinkling waters reflected the surrounding marble walls which still have their *pietra dura* dados and floral wall-paintings. One end is open, while a magnificent jali screen crosses the other, one of the Fort's finest surviving treasures. Its breathtaking and daringly lace-like carving is topped with an extraordinary panel of bold cartouches surrounding a semi-circular design of the scales of justice perched on a crescent moon amid billowing clouds and celestial bodies. Touches of the scarlet, blue and gold paintwork are still in place. The canal comes from the north side, where three more rooms make up the Tasbih-Khana (Chamber for Telling Beads), the Emperor's private place of worship. Here the simple portico stands between two small rooms decorated with mirror-work like that in Rang Mahal. The canal then flows into the southern portico, which is the width of the whole building and is softly lit through marble screens on the east and west sides and through five cusped arches on the south. Here it breaks its lines to make a large octagonal pool whose waters would have reflected the gold and brightly coloured floral paintwork coating every surface – lattice designs on the ceiling, panels and cartouches on the walls and friezes under

Above, as soon as it entered the Fort, the Nahr-i Bihisht was directed along this now grassy canal first to serve the royal Hammams and then to run through the private royal riverside palaces, cooling the air and reflecting in the mirrorwork and gilt decoration.

Below, architecture played an important part in the Persian char bagh. This pavilion, named Bhadaun, was added to the north end of Hayat Bakhsh, the Fort's largest garden. Built entirely of marble, with its columns and scalloped arches richly carved, it continues the high standards set by Shah Jahan's buildings.

the arches. This hall was known as Tosh-Khana (Robe Chamber) or Baithak (Sitting Room). Under the arch to Khwabgah, an inscription notes that building began in 1639, was completed in 1648 and cost 50 lakhs of rupees; it probably refers to all the palaces, not just this one.

But the Khas Mahal's most elaborately decorated room is the domed, semi-octagonal tower breaking the Fort's east wall. This is the Mussaman Burj (Octagonal Tower), also called the Jharokah-i Darshan (Showing Balcony), as it was from here that the Emperor showed himself to the people to let them know he was alive and well. Five sides of the tower have jali screens; the rest have their dado walls inlaid with luxurious *pietra dura*, which extends round the inside of the doorway arch, its highest flowers still bright with gems where stealing fingers have never reached. Paintings coat the remaining surfaces. The balcony, however, is an addition built in 1808-9 by Akbar Shah II, as is noted in an inscription above its arches.

The Khas Mahal has beauty and intimacy, and the Rang Mahal and Diwan-i-Am display an elegant grandeur. The Diwan-i-Khas (Private Audience-Hall) combines all these qualities. This is the finest building in the Red Fort, reflecting its position as the most important of the palace buildings. It was also the most expensive, constructed only in marble and costing Shah Jahan 1,400,000 rupees. This is where the Emperor held his special audiences to discuss his most important, sensitive and secret affairs. Here he sat upon his bejewelled Peacock Throne, in a marble pavilion whose lower walls were encrusted with agates, pearls, cornelians, lapis lazuli and other gem stones, and whose remaining surfaces were coated with golden paintings which still glow brilliantly as the sun lowers in the west. Again, the visitor's first encounter with the Diwan-i-Khas was controlled. In front of it was another enclosed courtyard, lined with small rooms. A corridor running from the north side of the Diwan-i-Am courtyard led to a single door in the centre of the west side. To gain entry, it was necessary first to do obeisance behind a red curtain; when inside, lesser nobles stayed in an outer enclosure and higher ones stood nearer the Emperor.

Thus the first view of the building was straight onto its west façade. The pavilion, measuring 980 by 67 feet, sits on a platform faced entirely with marble carved with budding floral cartouches and a band of lotus blossoms. A five-arch cusped arcade stands on square piers. The decoration on the arcade adds to the gentle rhythm of the large façade: the cusps are outlined to give emphasis; the corners are left blank to show off the carved cartouches on the pillars, which stretch right up to the eaves, dividing the arcade into five rectangles; and at the bottom of each pillar is a hint of the rich interior decoration to come, a panel of *pietra dura* inlay showing a large, blossoming plant within a border of floral arabesques. Above the arcade, the wall curves out gently to meet the deep chajja (eaves). Made of marble, it is crisper than the Diwan-i-Am's and so gives a sharper horizontal focus, emphasized by its own shadow beneath and by the broad and plain parapet above. The façade is completed by the corner roof-top chhatris, the final touch to give the building lightness and to match it happily with the Rang Mahal.

Inside the Diwan-i-Khas, all is measured luxury, showing off Shah Jahan's refined decoration. The floor is polished marble. Eight great piers form a wide aisle around a large central space; two more form the northern façade and a final four make three small central arches for the southern one. At the back of the pavilion, windows at floor level cool the air, each one set in a gilded and cusped blind arch. The Emperor's marble dais sits in front of the central, triple window; and so that his subjects could pay due respect without danger, the Nahr-i Bihisht flows underneath the marble floor of the central area. Restoration is revealing the original impact of the decoration, which must have dazzled first-time arrivals. Every surface is covered, and yet there is no hint of vulgarity. Piers are given *pietra dura* inlay below two carved floral cartouches; walls and arches have brightly painted and gilded floral swags; the cornice is a band of gilded chrysanthemums; the outer ceiling has lilies and roses while the central section has gold trefoils (which were repainted in 1911). Here, beneath the ceiling at the north and south ends, Shah Jahan had the renowned poet and saint Amir Khusrau's couplet inscribed: 'If on earth there be a paradise of bliss. It is this, Oh! It is this! It is this!'. (Khusrau, who died in 1325, was probably describing Siri, the Delhi of his day.)

In all, the palace displays a majestic weightiness which is absent from Shah Jahan's delicate and smaller Diwan-i-Khas built at Agra a decade earlier. There the slender double columns are merely outlined, while the decoration is concentrated on the capitals and bases; here at Delhi, the square columns of the massive pillars are the decorative focus. The whole building at Agra has jewel-fine lightness; the

The interior of Aurangzeb's tiny Moti Masjid is entirely of marble. It took five years to decorate, but although the carving is exuberantly baroque, the overall impression is one of devout chasteness. On the ground, each marble musalla is inlaid with a double outline of black and mustard-yellow polished limestones, while three floral sprigs provide the only touches of colour in the entire mosque. Above this, there is a riot of carving: a wall of flowers at the far end, vases of lilies in the squinches beneath the domes, and more vegetation meandering over the domes.

The restored painting on the marble ceiling of the Khas Mahal south portico glows with a bold and lively pattern of blue and white blossoms on gold and green entwining stems, criss-crossed by gold foliate lattice-work. Lit by sunlight filtered through thin, luminous marble, it gives a good idea of the delicate, almost feminine, character of the whole portico before the wall-painting faded.

overall effect at Delhi is one of supreme opulence in a refined and classical framework.

The buildings servicing palace life lie north of the Diwan-i-Khas. Nearest are the Hammams (Baths), now closed to the public. Hammams were a vital part of Islamic life – every Islamic community had a mosque, a market and a bath house. Thus, the Hammam is given almost palatial status. Its main door opens directly towards the Diwan-i-Khas; it has a prime riverside position; and it is built of marble and decorated with inlay, wall-paintings and stained-glass windows. The Nahr-i Bihisht supplied water to its three rooms: a changing room with fountains on the east side, a cold bath in the middle and a hot steam bath on the west side – as in Roman baths, this was a place where important political discussions took place. The floors of two rooms are remarkable. They are of white marble inlaid all over with *pietra dura*. In each, the lattice-pattern field encased in a wide border of bold flowing arabesques is like a great custom-made, wall-to-wall carpet. If it is difficult to recreate the former grandeur of the Red Fort's palaces, here is a glowing morsel that has survived until today, clearly visible if you peep through the windows.

West of the Hammams is the Moti Masjid (Pearl Mosque). The Red Fort was originally designed without a mosque: the Emperor and his Court went to the city's Jama Masjid. When pious Aurangzeb succeeded his father as Emperor, he found it inconvenient to go so far, and began this exquisite and aptly named private royal mosque in 1659. It took five years to build, measures just 40 by 35 feet and is made entirely of marble. Its triple domes were originally gilded with copper, and the somewhat constricted necks betray the change, if not the start of a decline, in architectural taste under Aurangzeb. As with the Khas Mahal, the exterior blind wall is articulated with square panels. Inside, the tiny courtyard is like a cube-shaped marble casket. Every detail is painstakingly worked on – each marble musalla (prayer carpet) is outlined in black marble; *trompe l'oeil* bowls of fruits and floral cartouches surround the entrance; the central pool had *pietra dura* inlay; fine yellow and black stripes outline the steps up to the sanctuary; bold, almost baroque, blossoms and piers with herringbone stripes break up the walls; slender minarets pierce the skyline. In the Inner Sanctum, every inch of wall and ceiling is carved, and the prayer spaces of the floor even have *pietra dura* inlay. The Moti Masjid

Inside the Hammams, all is regal luxury. The royal feet could step out of the grey marble bath onto a marble floor entirely inlaid with semi-precious stones, limestones and marbles, all gently lit by filtered sunlight. A closer look at one corner shows how refined and delicate the workmanship is, like the best French rococo decoration. Flower stems could not be finer, leaves are light and springy, and the individual petals of the central sunflower are outlined for emphasis.

This was the centre, the barahdari, of the geometric Persian garden.
In Shah Jahan's time it was a grand affair with more than 160
fountains. This one of sandstone was built by the last Mughal
emperor, Bahadur Shah II, with latticed windows to keep out the heat
and protect the ladies, and a causeway to reach it across the pool.
Leading up to it is one of the newly restored principal water-channels,
its fountains ready for action. The marble Bhadaun pavilion rises
behind, whose niches to brighten tumbling water can be seen through
the central arch.

takes Mughal refinement to a degree only possible on this small scale.

North of the Hammams and Moti Masjid lie the royal gardens. Like the baths, they were essential to Islamic life and especially to Mughal Court life. Babur missed his northern climate and laid out the first Persian garden in the punishing dust and heat of India. The garden was not just an oasis from the seering heat of the Delhi plain, but was also important as a royal pleasure garden and, perhaps more significantly, as a symbol of the paradise all Muslims hoped to achieve after life. So, in accordance with the Koran's description of paradise, the classic Persian char-bagh (four-garden) was enclosed by a wall and crossed by two channels dividing it into four areas, which were planted with species chosen for their flowers, fruits, leaves or morning and evening scents. The crossing was the most important area of the garden, and often had a pool and barahdari (summer house). The introduction of exotic fish and birds completed this earthly paradise.

Gardens were an integral part of Shah Jahan's new city – he built three outside the walls and one by Lahore Gate; his daughter Jahanara built Sahibabad and a second one in Chandni Chowk; his daughter Raushanara built another; his wives Nawab Akbarabadi Begum and Nawab Sirhindi Begum built still others; and nobles added more. The finest gardens were two, laid out side by side, inside the Red Fort. Hayat Bakhsh (Life-Giving) was the larger, Mahtab (Moon) the smaller (now covered by barracks). Hayat Bakhsh, whose southern wall skirted the Diwan-i-Am courtyard, Moti Masjid and Hammams, followed the classic Persian formula on a thoroughly royal scale (although the present layout is different). Its barahdari was said to have 49 silver fountains, its surrounding pool another 112, and yet more filled the canals. The main north–south avenue was later closed with two exquisite marble pavilions which cascaded water and were named after the monsoon months of the Hindu year, Bhadaun (fifth month, at the north end) and Sawan (fourth month). The pavilions are still standing, with their triple row of oil lamp niches behind the cascade, vestiges of inlay work and floral carving on the dado. All hint at the original quality of the whole garden. (By comparison, the Mahtab Bagh's highlight of a red stone barahdari must have seemed rather modest.) The barahdari is, however, now merely a red stone pavilion in the large tank, with a causeway to the garden, which was built by the romantic Bahadur Shah II in about 1842 and given his *nom de plume*, Zafar-Mahal.

The source of water to the gardens was again the Nahr-i Bihisht canal, which was ingeniously hauled up into the Fort at the north-east corner of Hayat Bakhsh, beside Shah Burj (King's Tower). Aurangzeb later gave the entry of the canal style by making its waters pour over a marble cascade and into an oval pond surrounded by bulbous columns. It then ran southwards along an elevated strip to the string of marble palaces, passing two small marble pavilions built by Bahadur Shah II: Moti-Mahal, now gone, and Hira-Mahal.

The life of the Red Fort did not end within its walls. As we have seen, there was a strong interdependence between the Fort and the city, and nothing was more symbolic of this relationship than the Jama Masjid (Friday Mosque), the principal congregational place of worship for the Court and the populace. The major Islamic services were held each week at the Jama Masjid. As with all mosques, the large courtyard was the central focus, with a pool for worshippers to wash hands and face. The roofed area at the western end contained the central mihrab (alcove), indicating the direction of prayer. The imam (religious leader) conducted the prayers and read the Koran from the pulpit on the right; the khatib (reader) delivered the sermon; the muezzin (crier) called the people to prayer from one of the minars (towers). There were often special areas for women, travellers and scholars.

Although the hillock site of the Jama Masjid was selected early on in the plans for the city, work began only after the Court had moved to Shahjahanabad. The foundation stone was laid on 6 October, 1650. At a cost of a million rupees, some five thousand diggers, stone-cutters, carvers, engravers, jewellers and painters built what is still one of the largest mosques in India. Ustad Khlil, the architect, further emphasized the site by building on top of a high plinth – the mosque was first named Masjid-i-Jahan Nama (Mosque with a View of the World). For materials he used glowing Fatehpur Sikri red sandstone, adding extravagant inlay of marble and brass. Two men oversaw the project, wazir Saadullah Khan and Fazil Khan, the khan samen (head of the household). Six years later the royal mosque was ready.

Three great flights of steps lead up to the courtyard, the north and south ones for the public and the east one for the Emperor to climb up from Khas Bazar, the royal processional route from the Red Fort. At the top of each flight, three high, double-storey gateways open into the courtyard. Different bazaars traded at the

Above, markets surround the steps of the Jama Masjid, as they did when it was built. Around these eastern ones, bird and clothes sellers still flourish, as in Shah Jahan's time.

Below, in the shadows of the Jama Masjid's southern gateway, Muslim traders continue to sell chickens, as did their forefathers. Not a morsel is wasted: while some birds look on their future fate, the shop-keepers pluck and chop up others.

Above, the great courtyard of the Jama Masjid measures a thousand square yards. Lady Emily Bayley stayed with her father, Sir Thomas Metcalfe, the Agent in Delhi, in 1848–57, and thought the Jama Masjid had 'none in India to equal it'. One year she watched the celebrations on the last day of Ramadan from the high gallery of one of the gateways: 'Nearly five thousand people stood shoulder to shoulder in the courtyard in pure white dress and turbans, and not a sound was to be heard save the voice of the officiating priest or Mullah who . . . sung out his address so that it could be heard at the furthest limit of the courtyard. When the call to prayer came, the whole of that vast crowd threw themselves on their knees and bowed their heads to the ground . . . and remained motionless until the prayer was ended'.

Below, the faithful swarming up and down the south steps of the Jama Masjid. Lady Emily Bayley concludes her account of Ramadan at the mosque with a description of the shoe system. 'When the crowd broke up and rushed out of the different gateways, no longer silent but jabbering at the pitch of their voices, another wonderful sight presented itself, for all these five thousand worshippers had left their leather shoes on the broad flights of steps outside the courtyard, and now they reclaimed them. It was always a puzzle to me how they could ever find their own footwear again, as the shoes lay side by side from the top to the bottom of the steps, and were almost all of the same pattern.'

bottom of each flight of steps: magicians and jugglers at the northern, kabab and chicken sellers at the southern, and cloth and pigeon dealers in Khas Bazar. The mosque's annexes were at ground level, too: a hospital funded by the Emperor to the north-west, a school to the south-west. Even from the exterior, the mosque was something quite different from Shah Jahan's almost contemporaneous Moti Masjid built inside Agra Fort. That is enclosed, personal, calm and refined, its pearl white interior discovered behind unobtrusive doors in a blank wall. In Delhi, Shah Jahan's chosen site instead followed Akbar's magnificent mosque at Fatehpur Sikri, which was set on the highest spot and accentuated by the great Buland Darwaza and Badshahi Darwaza gates reached up steep steps. And like Akbar's mosque, the Jama Masjid is separate from the palace.

The courtyard measures a thousand square yards, a huge and beautiful space. Marble lines the lower walls, there is a central pool, and gates, towers and minarets break the skyline. Domed pavilions punctuate the corners and a pillared corridor runs along three walls. On the east side, open arcading looks towards the Red Fort – such a strong visual relationship is absent from the great Badshahi Mosque, built by Aurangzeb in 1574 and within view of Lahore Fort. To the west lies the prayer hall, whose two tall, slender minarets and three black-and-white striped, marble onion domes dominate Old Delhi and are its landmark. The prayer hall has an eleven-arch façade of red sandstone outlined in marble inlay; inside, seven mihrabs are carved into the west wall.

In its design for both royal ceremonial and public worship, the Jama Masjid is a symbol of both Red Fort and city. Its enormous size coped with the vast imperial Court but did not compromise the quality of its architecture. Indeed it was perhaps the crowning achievement of Shah Jahan's remarkable city: other emperors built great mosques, but none matched the Jama Masjid at Delhi.

The faithful wash their hands and faces in the central pool of the
Jama Masjid's great courtyard before worship. Behind them, regular
visitors feed the pigeons; beyond, the walls of the Red Fort are just
visible through the arcade.

*The blank walls of the royaᵢ Hammams, with their simple blind
panelling, betray nothing of the wonder inside.*

A Better Future?

4

'The palace at Delhi is, or rather was, the most magnificent palace in the East – perhaps in the world . . . The gems of the palace [remain], it is true, but without the courts and corridors connecting them they lose all their meaning and more than half their beauty. Situated in the middle of a British barrack-yard, they look like precious stones torn from their settings in some exquisite piece of Oriental jeweller's work and set at random in a bed of the commonest plaster.' James Fergusson, *History of Indian and Eastern Architecture,* 1910.

When Fergusson was writing, the Red Fort was in the worst condition of its entire history. Today, there is at least interest in its architecture: eight to ten thousand people visit the Fort every day, and a popular 'sound and light' show is staged nightly in Hindi and English. Even so, the great palace at the centre of one of the world's grandest empires is arguably now in an even worse condition than when Fergusson saw it. Reduced to a handful of empty, unfurnished rooms on a tourist route, its new enemies are not armed soldiers but erosion, pollution and an archaic and uncommitted attitude to restoration and conservation. It is the rest of Shahjahanabad, the city outside, which continues to buzz; inside, the only hint of former liveliness is the Chatta Chowk, whose walls are lined with thriving tourist and art shops, some of them of well above average standard.

The demise of the Red Fort began early in its three hundred and fifty year history. Shah Jahan's blissful life in his dream city was short-lived. He had arrived in 1648, became ill nine years later, and his four sons began plotting for the throne. Dara Shukoh, the heir apparent and favourite, went with his ailing father to Agra and sent out armies to quell his siblings. Shah Shuja fled to Burma, but the third son, Aurangzeb, allied with the youngest, Murad Bakhsh, and defeated Dara Shukoh. Events moved fast. Aurangzeb imprisoned his father in Agra Fort, tricked Murad and had him murdered, and proclaimed himself Emperor in 1658. He then captured Dara Shukoh, had him executed in 1659, paraded his corpse down Chandni Chowk as a warning to local supporters, and again proclaimed himself Emperor. It was a bloody beginning to the long rule of the last Great Mughal. Meanwhile, Shah Jahan, the great builder, lived as a prisoner in Agra's Mussamun Burj, gazing across to the Taj Mahal until he went to join his wife there in 1666. On his gravestone are inscribed

The other Hammam rooms have miraculously survived to show just how luxurious a royal bath can be. The **pietra dura** *marble floor of mustard flower-heads set within a red and grey lattice framework is almost perfect, as are the surrounding borders of cartouches. Even the dado of spindly flowers retains some of its colour.*

the words: 'The illuminated and sacred resting place of Shah Jahan, Emperor . . . having his abode in paradise and his dwelling in the starry heavens, called Firdaus Ashyani [dwelling in paradise] who was born like Timur when Jupiter and Venus were in the same constellation and who was a valiant ruler . . .'.

The greatest Mughal spectacles, staged with style at vast expense against the backdrop of a specially built city, would soon decline. The Empire's stability and cultural apogee were over. Aurangzeb (ruled 1658-1707) spent little of his long rule at Delhi, although he was there long enough to add the Moti Masjid, and his daughter built the Zinat-ul-Masjid just south of the Red Fort. He and his successor, Bahadur Shah I (ruled 1707-12), spent most of their reigns campaigning in the Deccan. The prosperity and population of Shahjahanabad declined.

The city revived under a second set of emperors. Considerably less powerful and more decadent, their fast turnover reflected the downhill path of the Empire. In just forty-seven years, between 1712 and 1759, five emperors ruled a dwindling Empire from the Red Fort, indulging their artistic patronage in music, literature, mosques and gardens including, inside the Fort, some garden pavilions. It was now that wealthy but weak Delhi suffered a spate of internal unrest and external attacks. The city was sacked three times: the worst assault was made by the Persian, Nadir Shah, in 1739. His soldiers massacred Delhi's inhabitants and two months later carried off loot that included the royal jewels and the treasury, amongst it the Koh-i-Nur diamond and the Peacock Throne. He also took '1,000 elephants, 7,000 horses, 10,000 camels, 100 eunuchs, 130 writers, 200 builders, 100 masons' and more. After this, Emperor Muhammad Shah (ruled 1719-48) became a ghostly figure in the Red Fort, taking comfort in what the poet Dom Moraes describes as 'the marble pavilions, the splashy fountains, the resilient flesh of women and boys, the huge banquets'. Next, the Afghan, Ahmad Shah Abdali, came in 1757. And when the Rohilla, Ghulam Qadir Khan, arrived in 1788 he found Delhi a provincial city occupied by the Marathas and the Emperor reduced to a figurehead – the Marathas had removed the Diwan-i-Khas's silver ceiling in 1760.

However, throughout these upheavals, the fabric of the city and Fort survived virtually intact. Then, in 1803 the British, fighting for the East India Company, won Delhi. Building mainly north of the city but sometimes inside its walls, they

A party of Kashmiris, wrapped up in the warm clothes of their homeland, explore Delhi's most popular tourist attraction on a sunny winter's day.

The Diwan-i-Khas (above) and the interior of the Moti Masjid (below), both watercolours painted by Company School artists. The first shows clearly how the red awnings were hung from the façade and propped up with long red poles; more red awnings shaded and gave privacy to the Emperor as he moved between the Khas Mahal, Diwan-i-Khas and Hammams. The second emphasizes the rich, lace-like, marble carving which so impressed the British. Company School paintings have a particular place in Indian art. Between 1803, when the British took Delhi, and 1858, when direct rule by the Crown began, the city was governed by the East India Company. With the demise of Mughal patronage, Indian painters looked to the British, who energetically commissioned paintings, usually watercolours, to record the more romantic and exotic aspects of their temporary home, especially the fairytale buildings. The British writer and painter Emma Roberts noted that 'there is no place in British India which the intellectual traveller approaches with feelings more strongly excited than the ancient seat of the Mughal empire.'

established colonial control and used Delhi as a strategic base for diplomatic negotiations with the Rajput maharajas and the north-west Provinces.

The emperors, meanwhile, played out the sunset of the Mughal Empire in the Red Fort, surrounded by several hundred dependent relatives and hangers-on, minutely observing the Court ritual but bankrupt of all power and income. Bishop Heber, visiting Akbar Shah II (ruled 1806-37 and added the Khas Mahal balcony) in 1825, found wood stacked in the Diwan-i-Am, pipal trees growing out of the Diwan-i-Khas, the imperial throne encrusted with pigeon droppings, the precious stones stolen from the *pietra dura* work and 'walls stained with the dung of birds and bats. . . all was desolate, dirty and forlorn'. When Emily Eden, sister of the Governor-General of India, camped at Delhi in 1838, she found 'hundreds of the Royal family of Delhi who have never been allowed to pass these walls, and never will be. Such a melancholy red stone notion of life as they must have!' Equally sad was 'the king of Delhi's palace . . . so magnificent originally, and so poverty-stricken now . . . the old king [Bahadur Shah II] was sitting in the garden with a chowrybadar waving the flies from him; the garden is all gone to decay, and 'the Light of the World' had a forlorn and darkened look . . . in some of the pavilions there were such beautiful inlaid floors, but the stones are constantly stolen'. Miss Eden's conclusion is remarkably enlightened: 'In short, Delhi is a very suggestive and moralising place – such stupendous remains of power and wealth passed and passing away – and somehow I feel that we horrid English have just "gone and done it", merchandised it, revenued it, and spoiled it all. I am not very fond of Englishmen out of their own country.'

It was into this city that mutineers marched in May 1857 in the First War of Independence, also known as the Mutiny. The next year the emperor, Bahadur Shah II (ruled 1837–58), was deposed. His empire had been reduced to the thoroughly run-down Red Fort, where he had added the two pavilions along the eastern wall and one in the garden tank. He lived there as a prisoner until he was exiled to Burma; he died in 1862. The glorious Mughal Empire ended and the British Raj began.

But it began with what John Keay termed 'one of the blackest chapters in the history of Anglo-Indian relations'. The city was ransacked, the imperial palaces looted and mosques desecrated. Passions ran high. It was suggested that the landmark and symbolic Jama Masjid should be blown up, sold, converted into a barracks or, most tasteless of all, used as a Hall of Remembrance to victims of the war, the courtyard pavement inscribed with their names – British only, of course. There was even a proposal to flatten the whole of Shahjahanabad and start again.

After the British retook Delhi, they made the Red Fort their headquarters. Tragically, in 1858 they wilfully and unnecessarily devastated the great palace. A map made at the time and now in the Fort Museum reveals how former palaces served the military garrison. The Jilau Khana became Magazine Square, and malt liquor was stored just inside Lahore Gate. The string of marble palaces became soldiers' quarters (Mumtaz Mahal), a hospital (Rang Mahal; other maps give this function to Diwan-i-Am), officers' quarters (Khas Mahal and Diwan-i-Khas) and a cooking room (Hira Mahal – the British destroyed neighbouring Moti Mahal). The most pathetic label was affixed to a single, small room in the long bazaar running to Delhi Gate: 'ex king of Delhi'.

But it is the vast empty spaces which are the most horrifying element of the British destruction. In these once stood the harem, courtiers' homes, bazaars, courtyards and gardens. Almost eighty per cent of the Fort's buildings were destroyed, deliberately blown up to leave what were considered the 'isolated buildings of architectural or historical merit'. Even those lost the copper-gilt plating from their roof chhatris and their marble paving and colonnades to what were known as 'prize-agents'. The rape of the Fort was completed when Captain (later Sir) John Jones took the inlaid panels at the back of the Diwan-i-Am off to London and sold them for £500 to the Government, who put them on display at the newly opened Victoria and Albert Museum.

As Fergusson fumed: 'The whole of the harem courts of the palace were swept off the face of the earth to make way for a hideous British barrack, without those who carried out this fearful piece of Vandalism thinking it even worthwhile to make a plan of what they were destroying or preserving any record of the most splendid palace in the world.' Fergusson argues that the military excuse for this destruction does not hold up, since there was 'in the palace and Salimgarh ample space for a garrison, more than doubly ample to man their walls', and space for a large and 'better ventilated' barracks just outside the walls. But gutting the palace was both cheaper and less bother than building a wall round a new barrack-yard.

From then on, the palace was firmly called the Fort. Outside it, the British cleared a huge area 500 yards deep to the south and west as a field for artillery fire. To achieve this, they wiped out whole mohallas (local areas), havelis (courtyard houses) and bazaars, and paid the enormous sum of £90,000 in compensation. While the British lived north of Shahjahanabad in Civil Lines, the city became congested as trade and industry revived. But even this had its disadvantages. The arrival of the railway cut through the north-west corner of the Fort and spliced the city in half, isolating the northern part and increasing congestion, and resulting in trees being chopped down and gardens being built over. By the 1890s, the city was overflowing.

Delhi was once again irresistible as a capital, this time to the British. As former Lieutenant-Governor of Delhi, Jagmohan observed: 'The British rulers, notwithstanding alienation from the people of Shahjahanabad, could not but be dazzled by the imperial tradition of the city'. The signal for its pre- eminence came in 1877, when on 1 January Viceroy Lord Lytton held a durbar in Delhi to celebrate Queen Victoria becoming Kaisar-i-Hind (Empress of India). It was held here, rather than Calcutta, 'since no city in the British Empire was so fitted as Delhi for the assumption of sovereignty of India'. Exactly six years later, in 1903, Viceroy Lord Curzon held another to proclaim Edward VII the King-Emperor of India. In scenes of magnificence not equalled since Shah Jahan's time, the Red Ford was the setting for a parade and an investiture. A grand ball was held in the Diwan-i-Am, its supper served in the Diwan-i-Khas.

On 12 December, 1911, there was a third durbar. To an audience that included 562 bejewelled maharajas, the King-Emperor George V announced that the capital of India would move from Calcutta back to Delhi. The durbar was held north of Shahjahanabad, but the royal couple also visited the Red Fort. On 14 December, wearing glittering crowns and royal robes, they followed the Mughal example and waved to half a million of their subjects from the Jharokah-i Darshan; and the Diwan-i-Khas ceiling was repainted for the occasion. Not everyone was pleased by this decision: one Shahjahanabad resident made an attempt on Viceroy Lord Hardinge's life, which only resulted in the British making Chandni Chowk easier to survey by cutting down its trees and bricking up its canal.

It is a tribute to Shahjahanabad that it remained a symbol of power and prestige – the reasons given for moving the capital here were its 'geographical, historical and political' importance. And yet, again following tradition, another fresh city was built, designed by Sir Edwin Lutyens. As part of the celebrations at its inauguration in 1931, Viceroy Lord Irwin took his place at the Jharokah-i Darshan to watch an extraordinary pageant of painted elephants, camels and other Indian transport. The marble halls were once more a stage-set, this time for extracts from 'Madame Butterfly' and spectacular broadsword dancing by the Scottish Highlanders. But the historic relationship between fort and city was soon broken: to connect the old British Area, Civil Lines, with New Delhi, the north-south road from Kashmiri to Delhi gates was widened into a highway.

However, the Red Fort's life was not yet over. Sixteen years later, at midnight on 14–15 August, 1947, India won independence. The next day, India's first Prime Minister, Jawaharlal Nehru, made a speech to the teeming crowds in Chandni Chowk from Aurangzeb's barbican in front of Lahore Gate. The Maharani of Jaipur remembers that Nehru once said 'the most exciting time of his life' was 'when for the first time the Indian tricolour was raised over the Red Fort'. The tradition continues annually, and now the gateway's windows have been bricked up for security reasons. As for the Red Fort's few inhabitants, they live in the army barracks. Meanwhile the thriving city's population is roughly half a million, double what it appears to have been at the death of Shah Jahan. Furthermore, they live in considerably less space. The few remaining havelis (courtyard houses) are workshops and warehouses, and the tree-lined avenues and gardens are gone. Inhabitants now squeeze into spaces left over from the railway, the wide roads and the new (and inappropriate) high-rise office buildings near Turkman Gate.

After such a turbulent 350 years, the Red Fort cries out for assiduous conservation and restoration. The massive task was begun, albeit half-heartedly, more than a century ago. Even before the British destruction, the approach of certain enlightened individuals was one of active appreciation and well-meaning – if somewhat misguided – repair work on many Indian monuments. While Bishop Heber and Emily Eden bemoaned the decay, the first flame of conservation energy crackled into life. Major Robert Smith, artist and admirer of Mughal architecture, was Garrison Engineer from 1822 to 1830. His first job was to repair the Jama Masjid, whose dome had trees growing out of it and whose back wall bricks had been 'taken away by

Above, this charming riverside pavilion lit by early morning sunshine is Hira-Mahal, added by the last Mughal emperor, the poet Bahadur Shah II. Its pair, Moti Mahal, has not survived. Behind it, the drab, greystone British barracks rises where the royal garden, Mahtab Bagh, used to provide blossoms and water-cooled air. Although they stand some distance away, they are still totally out of scale with all the surviving Mughal buildings. Their great Victorian presence hangs heavily over the whole Fort, a constant reminder of the wholesale British destruction of the majority of Fort buildings. The romantic Lovat Fraser bemoaned its loss when he came in 1902: 'Where once were leafy bowers, the blunt square outlines of the British barracks. And at the entrance to the marble halls, quiet, alert, reliant, with ruddy English face, a young soldier of the Gunners.'

Below, with typical Mughal attention to detail, the water flowing down from the Bhadaun monsoon pavilion into the central canal is given interest with this triple row of marble, scalloped niches. At night, a tiny oil lamp would be lit in each one, to add sparkle to the waterfall.

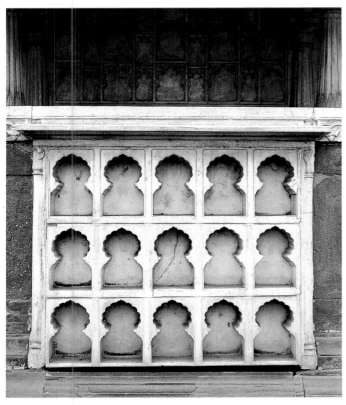

some heathen Hindoo to make himself a tenement'. After this and some less successful work on the Qutub Minar, he turned to the Red Fort, where he repaired the walls
– the interior, still the Emperor's territory, was out of bounds to him.

After the British vandalism of 1858, conservation energy sparked again towards the
end of the nineteenth century. In 1861, Lord Cunningham was appointed the first
Archaeological Surveyor, but his efforts were concentrated on earlier buildings than
the Red Fort and he had little backing from London. It was the arrival of Lord Curzon
as Viceroy in 1899 that marked the beginning of the Red Fort rescue operation.

Soon after his arrival at Calcutta, in an address to the Asiatic Society he summed
up the government's archaeological record for 'the most glorious galaxy of monuments in the world' as 'periods of supineness as well as activity . . . There have
been persons who thought that, when all the chief monuments were indexed and
classified, one might sit with folded arms and allow them slowly and gracefully to
crumble into ruin.' Within a year, Curzon had won from London the approval
to revamp the Archaeological Survey as an Archaeological Department run by a
Director-General as part of the imperial bureaucracy. Its responsibilities would be
for exploration, study and conservation of India's monuments and, most importantly,
it would have a budget. In 1902, the twenty-six-year-old Cambridge graduate John
Hubert Marshall arrived as first Director-General, a post he held for twenty-six
years. A law for protecting monuments was drafted, a staff including Indian scholars
was recruited and an ambitious scheme for systematic and continuous conservation
mapped out.

The new Department's success was, naturally, judged by its work on the Mughal
buildings of north-west India, especially in Lahore, Agra and Delhi. At the Red Fort,
Curzon's attention was drawn to the deplorable state of the palace buildings by a
Major Henry Hardy Cole, who in 1881 graduated from National Curator to the post
of Curator of Ancient Monuments. It is worth noting that Cole's job was to report
on what needed doing and to encourage repairs; it was not to conserve.

In 1903, the year of the second Delhi durbar, Curzon returned Fatehpuri Masjid
and Zinat-ul-Masjid to their congregations. The Red Fort, returned to the status of
palace monument, was cleared of some new military buildings and of lingering war
rubble. The stone elephants at Delhi Gate were renewed and some palace gardens

The Diwan-i-Khas was the setting for the tragic farces played out by later emperors who survived under East India Company government. In 1828, a certain Major Archer came here with the British Commander-in-Chief for an audience with Akbar Shah II. Riding right up to the courtyard in front of the palace through 'the squalid wretchedness of a most common village', they dismounted and entered through the famous red curtain. They then played out old court etiquette. 'We each made three salams or bows, . . . and a long lunged crier proclaimed that we came to see ''the king of the world''.'

The British party made their initial offerings which Akbar Shah carefully dropped into a basin. The Commander-in-Chief, given a royal turban and gown, dutifully presented more gold. More royal gifts produced more gold – but bestowing titles such as 'Ensign of the Fish' and privileges such as beating a drum when he marched in Delhi did not. The rest of the British party followed suit– 'about five-and-twenty people . . . How are the mighty fallen! The Emperor of Hindoostan a pensionary of a junta of merchants!.'

Above, the principal harem building, the Rang Mahal, was stripped of its silver roof by the Jats, used as a hospital by the British, and had the fabulous inlay of its marble fountain gouged out over the generations. But the less readily valuable mirror decoration of this and other little rooms known as Shish Mahals survives. But for how long, with pigeons nesting on every available perching place?

Below, royal visits often precipitate spring cleaning. And in honour of George V's visit here in 1911 the early champion of architectural preservation in India, Lord Curzon, repainted and regilded the magnificent ceiling of the Diwan-i-Khas, restoring the striking lattice-work patterning and the bold lily-flower border to its original colours.

restored, albeit incorrectly. By 1909, Curzon had scored another triumph: he had retrieved the inlay panels from London's Victoria and Albert Museum and, aided by Cole's earlier drawings and an Italian mosaicist, restored them to their original position in the Diwan-i-Am. Later, in preparation for George V's visit in 1911, Cole repainted the Diwan-i-Khas ceiling its original reds, blues and greens on gold ground, covering up an unfortunate earlier effort made in wrong colours (red, black and gold) and to the wrong design in honour of a visit by the Prince of Wales.

Worthy as the achievements of Curzon and his fellows were, there has been little development in the philosophy of the care of buildings in India since his time, particularly when compared to the advance in attitudes and techniques elsewhere in the world. After Independence, the Archaeological Survey of India, a government department within the Ministry of Culture, took over the responsibilities of India's monuments. The Red Fort is one in their care. The condition of the Red Fort today is a direct reflection of the attitude of its caretakers over the last forty years. It has been dominated by a piecemeal 'patch-up or close' approach, rather than a tackling of the fundamental problems with a comprehensive restoration programme. Nuggets of work have been carried out, each one carefully recorded in the annual *India Archaeology Review.* For instance, in 1956–7, the dead, porous concrete of the Diwan-i-Khas and Rang Mahal roofs was replaced; the following year, the Rang Mahal's underground cells were cleared of silt and flood-water and part of its marble floor was dismantled and re-set; and in 1959–60, work included repairing and cleaning the Diwan-i-Am balcony, cleaning and fixing the ceiling paintings of the Diwan-i-Khas and repairing the Rang Mahal sandstone floor.

The lists are precise, becoming longer and more alarming in 1964–5, when preparations for the 'sound and light' show involved a 'full face-lift'. This included the realignment of approach roads, repairs to pathways and floors, and coats of colourwash on the exterior of the Hammam, Diwan-i-Khas, Rang Mahal and other buildings. The marble surfaces of the Diwan-i-Khas, Moti Masjid and Bhadon pavilion were chemically treated. Alcohol and hydrogen paroxide helped remove stains from marble pillars, moss was scrubbed off exteriors, metal on the chhatris was cleaned and coated with a 'gold-coloured composition', and soot and grease were cleaned off the Diwan-i-Khas's painted floral decoration.

Most drastically, to give the audience a good view to the Diwan-i-Khas, trees were cut down or lopped, shrubberies turfed over and pathways realigned. Such a destructive face-lift is not the necessary price to pay for tourism. Plenty of historical knowledge exists to lay out the gardens closer to their original schemes and to indicate, albeit at ground level, the vast network of courtyards essential to understanding the character of the palace and appreciating its atmosphere. The sites of demolished buildings are known, too, and could be indicated.

But piecemeal repair work, and not much more, continues today. For instance, in 1975 the Rang Mahal fountain was made to work (it no longer does), and in 1983–4 bulging areas in the east wall were renewed with lateral and internal bonding. Meanwhile, certain actions positively harm the monuments and their setting. For instance, the army still occupies the barracks, despite Indira Gandhi's decision that it should be removed in phases, and despite the eminent conservationist Sir Bernard Fielden's endorsement that the army's removal was essential 'before adequate measures can be taken for conservation'. It was the army who won permission to build a huge water-tower near the Diwan-i-Am which is totally out of scale with the palace buildings and dwarfs their magnificence. Other piecemeal work has been equally damaging. New pathways not only give a false impression of the original layout, but their hard red gravel is carried on visitors' shoes into the buildings and ground into the marble floors. Lack of staff means the buildings are not patrolled and years of graffiti now coat the lower part of most walls; and it is not unusual to see a visitor using a coin to prize out a stone from the remaining *pietra dura*. Lack of basic maintenance means parrots are nesting in the Rang Mahal, pigeons leave their droppings in Khas Mahal's mirrored rooms, plaster is flaking off too many surfaces and gardens are minimally tended. As for the luxurious Hammams, they do survive together with their glorious floor decoration, fountains and baths, but are firmly closed to the public. Glimpsing them through the windows, their very survival is a silent rebuke for centuries of wanton destruction.

Added to these problems are the two most destructive forces, water and air. A hammering of humidity above and water below for 350 years has taken its toll, and continues to inflict more damage, including serious erosion to the walls and foundations of the riverside buildings. The problem is amplified by a water table

Above, before and after restoration. It is encouraging to see that the buildings of the great garden, Hayat Bakhsh are receiving attention. Just a few years ago, Bahadur Shah II's barahdari, Zafar Mahal, was in very poor shape; now the central balcony has been mended. But the superficial and inappropriate municipal flower planting in the tank cannot disguise the other parts of the building crying out for attention.

Below, before and after pollution. Two views of the back side of the Diwan-i-Am demonstrate the speed at which Delhi's increasingly high pollution is taking its toll on the surviving Red Fort buildings.

Above left, This flower, once a glowing masterpiece contributing to the elegance of the regal Diwan-i-Khas, has fared badly down the ages – less regal functions of the palace have included its serving as British officers' quarters. But it is the decoration's accessibility at ground floor level which has meant that greedy fingers, unchecked by custodians, have been able to prize out the coloured stones. Indeed, the panels are one of the most obvious recent casualties of the Red Fort, despite being under official protection. It is especially sad to discover that photographs of the same panels just twenty years ago show whole designs virtually intact.

Above, right, the changing room on the east side of the royal Hammams has an exquisite centralmarble fountain, surrounded by honey-coloured slabs. But the dado, once a glorious piece of delicate and colourful inlay, is now sadly bereft of almost all its stones. And the walls beg to be replastered.

Below, high up, out of the public reach (unlike the plundered Diwan-i-Khas decoration), this graceful cornelian flower is safe behind the throne of the Diwan-i-Am. In the panel to the right, the much-prized lapis pieces of the bird's tail-feathers and the flower petals have mostly survived, too; not so lucky were some green stone leaves, the cornelian of the surrounding flowers and the quatrefoils in the borders.

that rises and falls with the monsoons, the intermittent flooding of the Yamuna and extremes of cold and heat in the Delhi climate – the heat dries the bricks and encourages cracking. Furthermore, Delhi's increasingly polluted air, one of the world's worst, is also eating into the fabric.

Clearly, the Red Fort, magnificent as it was, has colossal problems today, compounded by the fact that seventeen government departments have an interest in it, which means most attempts at progress flounder in the bureaucratic mire. But the problems could be seen in a bright light. To begin with, the finest buildings of the Red Fort survive, despite atrocious and unforgivable losses. And the danger of what Fergusson considered the finest palace in the world becoming an increasingly dry archaeological site can be avoided. Its buildings need not gradually dissolve as atmosphere and time take their bitter toll, and its visitors can be given a better idea of what the complex originally looked like. There are a few optimistic administrators who speak of plans to revive the water system, of excavating tanks, of relaying gardens.

But, as everywhere, the time, money and effort needed for the job may be considered too great. It would be easier to keep the status quo, making such excuses as lack of finances, demands of other monuments, lack of manpower. The least acceptable excuse of all would be that major restoration requires the Fort to be closed to the public for a period and that this would not be possible. In the long run, the public would of course benefit from such a temporary inconvenience: their heritage would be richer and better cared for. The challenge to future custodians of the Red Fort, one of the 'most glorious galaxy of monuments in the world', is to check further decay by taking advantage of conservation and restoration progress in other parts of the world and making use of new approaches and techniques. Such foreign expertise has been offered to India, as well as funds to finance it. With her commercial wealth, funds for such a prestigious project would surely be easy to raise within India, too. A comprehensive programme for the Red Fort could be instigated and future generations enjoy to best advantage the remains of the centre-piece of Shah Jahan's great city.

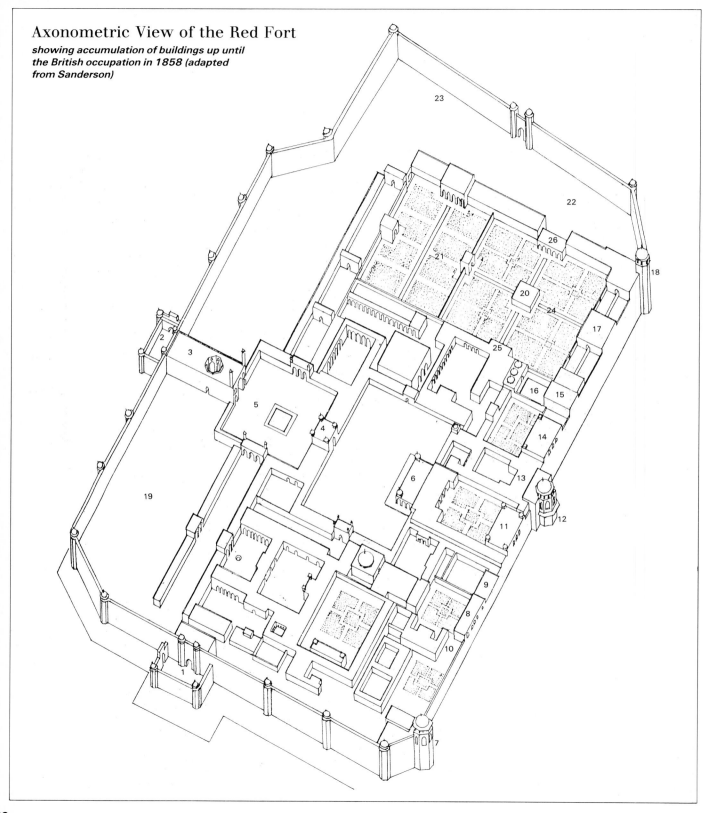

Axonometric View of the Red Fort
showing accumulation of buildings up until the British occupation in 1858 (adapted from Sanderson)

The Red Fort
adapted from Sanderson

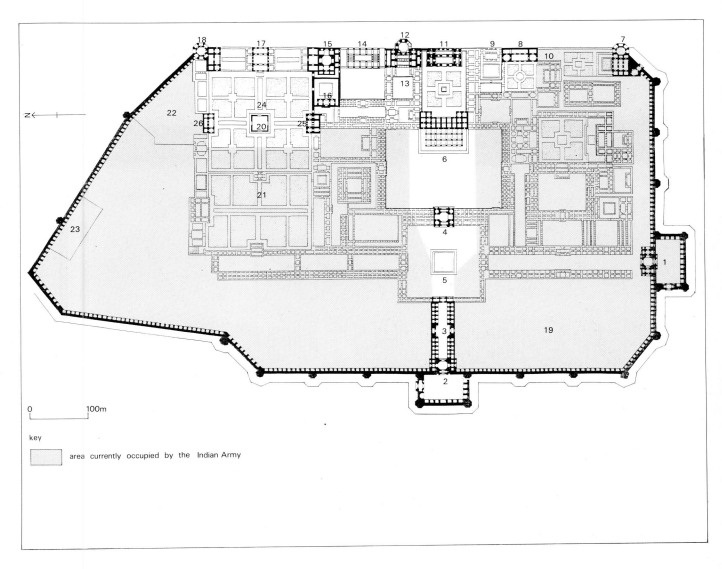

key

area currently occupied by the Indian Army

0   100m

key

1 Delhi Gate	**10** Kwaspura	**19** Common Houses
2 Lahore Gate	**11** Rang Mahal	**20** Zafar's Pavilion
3 Chatta Chowk Bazaar	**12** Musamman Burjh	**21** Mehtab Gardens
4 Naqqar Khana	**13** Khas Mahal	**22** Princes' Quarters
5 Jilau Khana	**14** Diwan-i-Khas	**23** Stables
6 Diwan-i-Am	**15** Hammams	**24** Hayat Baksh Garden
7 Asad Burj	**16** Moti Masjid	**25** Sawan Pavilion
8 Mumtaz Mahal	**17** Moti Mahal	**26** Bhadon Pavilion
9 Darya Mahal	**18** Shah Burj	

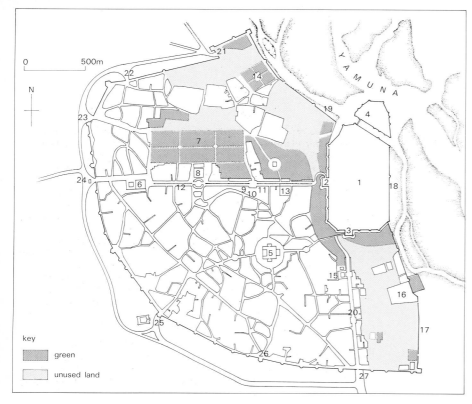

Shahjahanabad

Above: during the Mughal Period.

Below: (Old Delhi) today.

key

1   The Red Fort (Lal Qila)
2   Lahore Gate
3   Delhi Gate
4   Salimgarh Fort
5   Jama Masjid
6   Fathepuri Masjid
7   Begum Ka Bagh
8   Sarai
9   Sonheri Masjid
10   Kotwali
11   Gurudwara Shish Ganj
12   Chandni Chowk
13   Nahr-i Bihisht
14   Dara Shukoh Palace
15   Akbarabadi Masjid
16   Ghatta Masjid
17   Raj Ghat
18   Qila Ghat
19   Nigambodh Ghat
20   Faiz Bazaar
      City Gates:
21   Kashmiri
22   Mori
23   Kabuli
24   Lahori
25   Ajmeri
26   Turkman
27   Delhi (Akbarabadi)
28   St James' Church
29   Residency
30   Magazine Square
31   Railway Station
32   Town Hall
33   Baptist Church
34   Begum Samroo Palace
35   Daryaganj
36   Interstate Bus Terminus
37   Netaji Subhash Chandra Marg
38   Ramlila Ground
39   Ring Road

key

green

unused land

Travellers' Information

Open daily, sunrise to sunset, except on 15 August, Independence Day, and on rare occasions when a special national event is held there. Entrance at Lahore Gate; entry tickets are sold from the kiosk outside Lahore Gate, on the left side; 50 paise entry charge, free on Friday. The most magical times to visit the Fort are early morning (also the best time to look up at the palaces from outside the east wall) and late afternoon. The most crowded times are Fridays, when entry is free, and weekends — but Sunday has the jolly nearby street market sprawling all over Chandni Chowk. Coach tours tend to arrive mid-morning and mid-afternoon. It is worth allowing two hours even to visit briefly; the serious visitor would need much longer, and could join locals picnicking on the lawns. A good route to follow is first to wander Chatta Chowk, to imbibe a little atmosphere of the Fort's former bustle; then to explore the remaining palace buildings of Naqqar Khana, Diwan-i-Am, the string of riverside palaces from the Archæological Museum up to the Hammams, the tiny Moti Masjid and then the gardens.

There are two small museums inside the Red Fort: The Indian War Memorial Museum *in the Naqqar Khana and the* Archæological Museum *in Jahanara Bagum's Mansion (also known as Mumtaz Mahal). Red Fort relics include glass, porcelain and maps. Both open Saturday-Thursday, 10 a.m.-5 p.m.*

The Sound and Light show, delightful and very well done, is run by the ITDC (India Tourism Development Corporation). It fulfils its promise that '360 years of history comes alive' and is performed nightly in English and Hindi. Tickets cost Rs8 and are sold on the right side of the Naqqar Khana, inside the Red Fort. English timings are February-April 8.30 p.m., May-August 9 p.m., September-October 8.30 p.m., November-January 7.30 p.m.; the show lasts one hour; Hindi performances are 90 minutes earlier than English ones.

To photograph in the Red Fort, no permissions are needed for a hand-held camera. Permission for other filming may be obtained from the Director, Archæological Survey of India, Janpath, New Delhi (tel: 3012058). This takes time and requires form-filling.

The Red Fort visitor is often approached by freelance guides who have variable skills in English, history and recounting a good story. He is under no obligation to accept a guide but, if he does, should agree a price before setting off. The Survey's official guidebook is Y. D. Sharma's Delhi and Its Neighbourhood, *which provides reliable information accompanied by a useful plan.*

The shops in Chatta Chowk serve both tourists and locals, especially the art and antique shops such as Tula Ram, Mehra's Art Palace and Gulzari Lal's, all at the end on the right. Soft drinks, tea and snacks are sold here, and there is a pleasant café among Gulzari Lal's wooden rocking horses and great brass camels and elephants. Beyond the bazaar, beside the Naqqar Khana, Kerala Cafe has cold drinks and fruit juices. Behind the Diwan-i-Am there is a small drinks stall, and to the west of the Moti Masjid there is a tea and drinks café with seats. Here there are also lavatories, and there are more at the far north and south (beside the Museum) ends of the Fort.

Jama Masjid

Open to Muslims at all times, to non-Muslims at restricted times which vary but currently include prayer times. These change according to the lunar calendar. For example, the mosque is usually open to non-Muslims in March at 7 a.m.-12.30 p.m. (closing at noon on Fridays), 2 p.m.-4.45 p.m. and 5.15 p.m.-6 p.m.; these times would move earlier in summer, later in winter.

Entry is up the north or south steps; at the top, visitors leave their shoes or rent shoe-covers (giving a tip on leaving). Visiting the mosque is free; there is a charge of Rs2 for a hand-held stills camera and Rs10 for movie camera or a tripod. It is well worth climbing the south-west minaret to enjoy the superb view. It is open to all, regardless of faith, but women and children must be accompanied by a man. Stills cameras are permitted, but not movie cameras or, sadly, binoculars. Timings are 9 a.m.-6 p.m. daily, but not at prayer times; charges are Rs2 per person, and Rs2 per camera.

Staying in Delhi

Transport

The easiest way to move around central Delhi is by autorickshaw, agreeing a price in advance if the meter does not work; Delhi taxis usually have working meters. For autorickshaw or car, the driver will wait for visits to be made, charging Rs10 per hour waited. Within the lanes of Old Delhi, even down wide Chandni Chowk, a bicycle rickshaw is best, walking even better; a car is useless.

Hotels

The following selection are all convenient for Old Delhi, listed in descending order of price. There is a perpetual bed shortage in Delhi, so it is wise to book.

● Taj Mahal Hotel, 1 Mansingh Road, New Delhi 110011 (tel: 3016162; telex: 66874/61898 TAJD IN; fax: 301 7299). Top of the market.
● Ashok, 50-B Chanakyapuri, New Delhi 110021 (tel: 600121; telex: 65207/65647). Deluxe, built in 1954 with Raj spaciousness.
● Imperial, Janpath, New Delhi 110001 (tel: 3328511; telex: 62603). Very central, stylish 1930s building and lawns.
● Oberoi Maidens, 7 Sham Nath Marg, Delhi 110054 (tel: 252464; telex: 66303). Just north of Old Delhi, built to serve the British in Civil Lines.
● Ambassador, Sujan Singh Park, New Delhi 110003 (tel: 690391; telex: 3277). More Raj spaciousness.
● Hotel Marina, 659 Connaught Circus, New Delhi 110001 (tel: 344658). Excellent location, clean and good value.
● Nirula's Hotel, L Block, Connaught Place, New Delhi 110001 (tel: 352419). Again, excellent location, clean and good value.

Restaurants

The following serve rich Mughlai cuisine enjoyed by the Mughals and with an emphasis on meat dishes:

In Old Delhi: Karim, on the south side of Jama Masjid, the best for food and atmosphere; Moti Mahal, Daryaganj, with evening ghazel singers; Jewahar, by Jama Masjid; Flora, Urdu Bazar, by Jama Masjid; Maseeta, by Jama Masjid.
In Connaught Circus: Degchi, 13 Regal Building; Minar, L11 Connaught Place; Mughlai, M17 Connaught Circus.

Eating in hotels: Mayur, Maurya Sheraton Hotel; Darbar, Ashok Hotel (good buffet); Haveli, Taj Mahal Hotel; Gulnar, Janpath Hotel (with Indian singing).

The following are excellent and convenient for snacks, drinks and full meals of Indian, Continental or Chinese cuisines: Nathu's, Bengali Market (east of Connaught Circus); Nirula's Hotel and the Imperial Hotel (see above); The Tea Room — Aap ki Pasand, 15 Netaji Subhash Marg, opposite the Golcha Cinema (here you can sample and buy India's best teas). For Chandni Chowk street snacks, Gantiwalla and Annapurna are two of the best sweatmeat shops and also sell savouries, while Naim Chand Jain, a blue-tiled kiosk on the south side, sells hot, sweeter-than-sweet jalebis all day long. At the bottom of the street, delicious fresh nuts and dried fruits are sold straight from the sack around Fatehpuri Masjid, and in the road running north from here Giani Ice-Cream sells not just ice-cream but also hot spiced cashewnuts and two irresistible hot halwas, carrot and dhal.

Shopping

Upmarket hotels have good in-house shops which keep long hours. Connaught Circus is the main area for all practical shopping and airlines, travel agents, etc. For books, Book Worm, 29-B Connaught Place and Oxford Book and Stationery Co at Connaught Circus; chemist, Kemp & Co, E-Block, Connaught Circus, or the medical stores in Super Bazar, Connaught Circus, which remain open 24-hours every day; photography/film, Mahatta & Co, 59-M Connaught Place; shoes, Metro, 16-F Connaught Place and Bata, D-4 Connaught Place.

To buy the astounding India craftsmanship, ranging from silks and sandalwood to bedspreads and brass boxes, the best place to begin is the Central Cottage Industries Emporium on Janpath, just south of Connaught Circus, a huge choice of quality goods from all over India at fixed prices; the next place to explore is the string of individual state emporia, also with fixes prices, in nearby Baba Kharak Singh Marg.

For off-beat shopping, Chandni Chowk is worth a stroll; at the far end, find excellent nuts, dried fruits and pickles around Fatehpuri Masjid; around Jama Masjid, fireworks; in Dariba Kalan running between Chandni Chowk and Jama Masjid, traditional Delhi crafts — gold and silver jewellery sold by weight, atta (perfume); and all tinsel, brocade, turbans, plumes and masks for weddings and festivals in Kinari Bazar. The cleverly designed, multi-layered tiffin cans used by Indians for their home-cooked picnic lunches eaten in the Delhi parks can be bought in various sizes in Chandni Chowk hardware stores.

The following provide information, maps, guides, tours and transport for the Red Fort and Old Delhi.
- Government of India Tourist Office, 88 Janpath (tel: 3320005)
- Delhi Tourism Development Corporation (DTDC), N-36 Connaught Place (tel: 3313637/3315322)
- India Tourism Development Corporation (ITDC), L-Block, Connaught Circus (tel: 3320331/3322336)
- American Express, A-Block, Connaught Place (tel: 3324119; telex: 62781/66420)
- SITA World Travel, F12 Connaught Place (tel: 3311133/3311122)

For further in-depth information on Old Delhi, both past and present, together with information on architectural walks, contact Madhu Bajpai, Secretary, Delhi Conservation Society, N-7/c Saket, New Delhi 110017 (tel: 668118); or Martand Singh, Secretary, INTAC, 71 Lodi Estate, New Delhi, 110003 (Tel: 611362).

Further Reading

Alexander, M., Delhi & Agra, A Travellers' Companion, *London, 1987*

Barton, G. and Malone, L, Old Delhi, 10 Easy Walks, *Delhi, 1988*

Davies, P., Penguin Guide to the Monuments of India, *vol. 2, Islamic, Rajput and British buildings, London 1989*

Dayal, M., Rediscovering Delhi: The Story of Shahjanabad, *Delhi, 1982*

Fanshaw, H. C., Shah Jahan's Delhi Past & Present, *Delhi, 1902 and 1979*

Frykenberg, R. E., ed., Delhi Through the Ages: Essay in Urban History, Culture and Society, *Delhi, 1986*

Gascoigne, B., The Great Moghuls, *London, 1971*

Gupta, N., Delhi between Two Empires 1803–1931, *Delhi, 1981*

Haig, W. and Burn, R., The Cambridge History of India, *vol. IV, 'The Mughal Period', London and Delhi, 1957 and 1987*

Kaul, H. K., ed., Historic Delhi: An Anthology, *Delhi, 1985*

Mason, P., ed., Historic Delhi: An Anthology, *Delhi, 1985*

Sharma, Y. D., Delhi and Its Neighbourhood, *New Delhi, 1974*

Singh, K. and Rai, R., Delhi, A Portrait, *Delhi, 1983*

Spear, P., Delhi, A Historical Sketch, *London, 1937*

Spear, P., A History of India, *vol. 2, London, 1978*